RAILWAYS THROUGH THE AGES

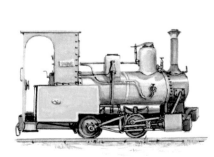

Half title: A variety of narrow gauge industrial locomotives that were used in many industries.

Above: Industrial railways of standard gauge commonly used green as a popular livery for locos.

Right: Flying Scotsman, No. 4472, leaving King's Cross Station for its journey north on the East Coast main line, with to the right background, its neighbouring station of St Pancras and its stylish 'gothic' hotel.

Railway Heritage

RAILWAYS THROUGH THE AGES:
A Selection of Industrial and Passenger Railways Past and Present

John Legg and Ian Peaty

Silver Link Books

Dedicated to our wives, Rosemary and Norma, for their tolerance over our obsession with railways both at home and abroad.

First published in Great Britain in 2023
by Silver Link Books
an imprint of Mortons Books Ltd
Media Centre
Morton Way
Horncastle LN9 6JR
www.mortonsbooks.co.uk

ISBN 978 1 85794 597 3

The right of John Legg and Ian Peaty to be identified as the authors of this work has been asserted in accordance with the Copyright, Designs and Patents Act 1988.

About the authors

John and Ian have been good friends for 60 years, which started when both of their wives worked at the same life assurance company in South Woodford. Since then they have raised their families, worked hard and of course, now retired. They have always had a great interest in railways, but work and family commitments severely reduced the time they could spend pursuing railways until the latter years.

Ian worked in the brewing business for many years, using his knowledge to write his first book published in 1985 called *Brewery Railways* followed by others including *Iron Rails and Whisky Trails* in 2013 and *Stone by Rail* in 2014, which describes rail-connected quarries.

Co-authors Ian Peaty, left, and John Legg. Friends for 60 years.

John was then retired and they discussed jointly writing a railway book, pooling their resources, as the four of them were taking regular holidays in various parts of the world with railways in mind, of course, and had accumulated many unique photographs and much research. The resulting book was called *A World of Rail* and was published in 2017. This was followed in 2020 by *Running on Rails*, which was UK based, both published by Silver Link. This current book, *Railways Through The Ages*, is similarly themed. Enjoy!

Contents

Private Owner Wagons

A selection of six private owner coal wagons owned by some of the numerous collieries and stone quarries that operated in The Forest of Dean, Gloucestershire.

Replica of Richard Trevithick's 1804 locomotive that pre-dated Stephenson's *Rocket* by some 25 years. It is seen here at the Iron Bridge Museum in Shropshire during 2009.

Railways in the UK have always attracted both ridicule and affection in equal proportions since the days of 'railway mania' in the 1840s when investment into railway lines escalated, fuelled by the promise of investment shares returning untold wealth to the speculators. Unfortunately there was no government control over the shaping of our railway network, resulting in a bizarre

A small industrial Kerr Stuart 'Wren' Class 0-4-0T locomotive *Lorna Doone* built in 1922 working at the Devon County Council Wilmington Quarry near Tavistock. It was one of three with *Peter Pan* and *Pixie*.

A GWR Class 4200, 2-8-2T No. 4247 built in 1916 now in preservation at the Bodmin and Wenford Railway, seen here in 2010 at Bodmin station.

situation of different private companies constructing their own lines often running almost parallel to their competitors and small branch lines that could never be prosperous. The investors, who were not only the wealthy landowners, merchants, bankers and parliamentarians, but also the better off general public, were all seemingly beguiled into this heavily promoted 'foolproof' risky venture. Often the general public did not have sufficient assets to counter any losses and could only afford the deposit.

By 1846 around 272 Acts of Parliament had been passed to set up new railway companies with proposed routes totalling 9,500 miles. It is estimated that only a third of these actually started to get built; others collapsing with no funds. Still others were bought out by larger competitors or companies set up in the name of building a railway, but used instead as a fraudulent means of diverting the hapless investors' money into some other enterprise.

Needless to say the collapse of the railway bubble was inevitable and when it came many

A Gresley designed A4, 4-6-2 No. 60026 *Kestrel* entered service for LNER on the East Coast Main Line in 1937 on the Kings Cross-Edinburgh route. The name was changed to *Miles Beevor* in 1947.

Southern Region (SR) Lord Nelson Class 4-6-0 No. 850 *Lord Nelson*, designed by Richard Maunsell built at Eastleigh in 1925 and seen here in preservation pulling into Headcorn station, Kent in July 2007. They were originally introduced for the boat train traffic to Dover and Folkestone.

investors lost everything as companies called in their dues. One of the leading protagonists was George Hudson, a politician and financier, who became known as the 'Railway King' and controlled a significant number of railways, especially in the Yorkshire area. He is reported to have used shareholders' cash to have his own station built on the York to Beverley Railway that bordered his Londesborough Hall estate. Unfortunately, his dubious financial practices with his shareholders' money ended in bankruptcy when the bubble burst.

In spite of these financial calamities, the UK was nevertheless left with 6,220 miles of serviceable track. In the years that followed and up to the beginning of the First World War in 1914 the network increased to 23,440 miles. This was reduced between the First and Second World War by some 1,300 miles due to the increase in road transport. There were more than 120 railway companies by 1923, when these were amalgamated under the 1921 Railways Act into four companies: Southern Railway, Great Western, London Midland and Scottish, and London and North Eastern Railway. The government of the day hoped that this would stem the losses and reduce inter-company competition.

After the Second World War the network was tired and run down, many more branch lines were closed and the big four companies were financially struggling, which forced the government to nationalise the industry in 1948, naming it British Railways. During the 1950s the railways continued losing money, with freight being gradually transferred to road transport and the government pouring increasing amounts of public money into the loss-making organisation.

A modernisation plan set out in 1955 looked at replacing steam locomotives with diesel and electric traction, but the losses just increased. A radical solution had to be found. This was provided by ICI's Dr Richard Beeching who joined the British Railways Board with a government remit to cut the losses and improve efficiency.

Between 1960 and 1965, Beeching assessed the remaining 18,000 miles of track and came up with two reports which identified 2,363 stations and 6,000 miles of routes and branch lines that were considered expendable. He also indicated that more use of containerisation for rail freight was necessary and that major trunk routes should be developed. There were protests from many areas and Beeching's plans became known as 'The Beeching Axe'. A few lines and stations were reprieved, but most of his recommendations were endorsed by the government.

An 0-4-2T locomotive built by W.G. Bagnall No. 3050 in 1953 for the 2ft (610mm) gauge railway of Rustenburg platinum mine of South Africa. It is now in preservation at the Welsh Highland Railway in Porthmadog, North Wales.

BR were still building steam locomotives to standard designs during this period, while on the Continent lines were mainly being constructed and converting to overhead electric traction, with good use of diesel locomotives being made where necessary and steam quickly disappearing from the scene.

Although a few diesel locomotives were built for, and run by, BR between 1948 and the early 1950s, no large scale manufacturing took place. It wasn't until the Modernisation Plan of 1955 that diesels for mainline duties were rushed into operation in greater numbers. Unfortunately many suffered reliability problems and were in service only a short while. The last steam locomotive built by BR in Swindon Works was a Class 9F 2-10-0, No. 92220 *Evening Star*, in 1960, but by this time all steam services were being replaced by more reliable diesel and electric traction. Steam services ceased completely after the last BR passenger service, the Fifteen Guinea Special, in August 1968 (£15-15 shillings = £15.75p).

During this time there were still private railways operating, but these were mainly industrial and operating within the confines of their company boundaries. They were a mixture of standard gauge, 4ft 8½in (1,435mm) and various narrow gauges and operated in breweries, quarries, distilleries, private estates,

collieries, docks and other manufacturing facilities. Most have now disappeared into the annals of history.

During the ensuing years the BR workforce was drastically reduced in line with the requirements of the new technologies; diesel and electric locomotives were more efficient and reliable. Electric signalling was becoming the norm and more centralised, and the short lengths of track were being gradually replaced by long lengths of welded rail to give a quieter and more comfortable ride for the passenger. In 1976 the High Speed Train (HST) was introduced on the Western Region from London Paddington to Bristol at 125mph. A total of 197 power cars were built and some are still in operation around the network, especially in Scotland.

Privatisation came along in 1996, putting an end to nearly 50 years of British Rail. Private companies now competed for franchises to run trains on the main routes and their branches. The railway infrastructure, such as track, signalling and stations was to be the responsibility of a new public body called Railtrack – although maintenance was contracted out to private companies; not always with the best safety records.

New rolling stock in colourful liveries replaced a considerable amount of old BR stock

Four LMS Stanier locomotives at an unknown shed in the early 1950s. The one on the extreme left is an unknown number; next on the right is Derby built 45660, Jubilee Class 4-6-0 named *Rooke*. Then Vulcan Foundry-built 45045, Class 5MT, 4-6-0 and finally Armstrong Whitworth built 45345 another 5MT. All locomotives were built during 1934.

with new suburban and long distance multiple unit trains. In 2006 the government launched an enquiry into the perennial railway problem of escalating costs, this time partly caused by the fallout from horrific accidents at Hatfield and Potters Bar and partly by increasing maintenance costs and reduced maintenance skills in Railtrack. This resulted in Railtrack being replaced by Network Rail, a non-profit company where any profit was to be used

for the benefit of the business. It is, in fact, a case of renationalisation. However, this is to be taken one step further by 2023 to become Great British Railways (GBR), a state-owned public body that will set timetables, sell tickets in England and manage rail infrastructure. It will also issue contracts to private operators.

At the time of writing, we have the Channel Tunnel and Eurostar operating to London St Pancras on the High Speed 1 line

BR Standard Class 9F, 2-10-0 No. 92203 *Black Prince*, built at Swindon in 1959 just before *Evening Star*, the last 9F and the last steam locomotive to be built for BR. It is seen here in preservation at the Cranmore 150 Quarry Gala Weekend, Somerset, in June 2008.

This is a fine example of a beautifully restored Class 33 diesel No. 33063, *R.J Mitchell*, designer of the Spitfire. A total of 98 were built by the Birmingham Carriage and Wagon Co. between 1960-1962 and nicknamed 'Cromptons' as electrics were installed by Crompton Parkinson. Now resident on the Spa Valley Railway and seen here at Eridge station in Kent.

A 1979 photo of Class 37 diesel electric locomotive, 37132, passing through Treeton in South Yorkshire hauling a train of mainly coal. A total of 309 were built between 1960 and 1965 as part of the BR modernisation scheme and were nicknamed 'tractors' because of the industrial sound of the engine.

Three GB Railfreight type 73 electro-diesel locomotives, 73962, 63 and 65 at their North Tonbridge yard in 2017 being readied for their next work assignments. After at least 50 years' service (1965) they are still widely used especially in the south where freight from outside enters the third rail 750 Volt DC network. A total of 49 were built at Eastleigh and Vulcan Foundry.

A First Great Western
HS 125 diesel at
Paddington station in
2016 just arrived from
Bristol Temple Meads.
197 of Class 43 were
built between 1975 and
1982. Capable of 125mph
(201kph) there was a
power car at each end
of the train. These trains
have served East Coast,
East Midlands, Grand
Central, Cross Country
and the Network Rail
Measurement trains.

Eurostar trains are
the international link
between the UK and
the rest of Europe from
St Pancras station,
down the HS1 line to
Folkestone then under
the English Channel to
France, Belgium and the
Netherlands. The service
was started in 1994 and
there are 11 Class 373
and 17 Class 374 train
sets travelling at 199mph
(320kph).

Tornado seen here in
June 2011 is a brand
new locomotive built as
an LNER Peppercorn,
4-6-2 Class A1 No.
60613 in 2008. It was
the first locomotive to
be built since the last
BR locomotive, *Evening
Star*, in 1959. Seen here
hauling a day excursion.

across to Paris and Brussels and now to Amsterdam. Stations have been upgraded and rebuilt, especially London Bridge, providing a more efficient service to London commuters, the Great Western line from Paddington to Bristol being part electrified and many more improvements around the UK. Another High Speed line, HS2 is currently under construction from London going north to Birmingham and beyond in the future.

This book provides an overview of some of the industrial, passenger and heritage railways of the past and present.

Class 66 in pristine livery hauling equally attractive new Tarmac bogie hopper cement tank wagons out of Tunstead cement works in the Peak District.

The last of 700 Class 66 No. 66779 manufactured by EMD in Illinois USA in 2015. It has nostalgically been named *Evening Star* after the last steam locomotive to be built for BR. It also displays the shed plate of 82F, Bath Green Park where it was last based. A traditional American warning bell is fitted to both ends of the locomotive.

Ind Coope Ltd Brewery showing both Midland Railway and Great Northern Railway wagons with one on its own having bow ends and two covered wagons with sliding hatches. The Ind Coope brewery is at the back with tall chimneys with the wooden casks (barrels) in front. The signal in front of the single wagon is an early double arm type that would be manually operated to lower and raise each arm.

Messrs. Ind Coope & Co's Brewery   Burton-on-Trent

Burton-on-Trent in Staffordshire is a pleasant market town situated on the River Trent, but it has a remarkable past.

Brewing beer had become the major occupation in the town by the early 1700s, as beer could then be transported down the Trent

Navigation to Hull, London and the Continent and around the country using the canal network. The number of breweries had only increased by the 1800s and in 1839 the Midland Railway (MR) came to Burton from Birmingham and the premier brewers were

At Truman's Brewery a four-wheeled wagon, No. B749034 specially built at BR Works Derby in 1950 to transport two detachable beer tanks firmly secured in place by adjustable chains connected to the individual cradles. The tank on the left has a vacuum device fitted to it just under 'No. 3 Tank'.

A line of Ind Coope locomotives outside the former Allsopp engine shed. At the front is a four-wheeled battery powered English Electric locomotive No. 9 built in 1922. It was first deployed at the Ministry of Munitions, Bramley Depot, in Hampshire and then in 1946 went to Allsopps/ Ind Coope. It was scrapped in 1968. The Sentinel steam loco, 0-4-0 VBGT, No.7, works No. 9376 was built in 1947 for Ind Coope/Allsopps and was sold in 1960. It has had a few owners since and is now in preservation.

quick to take advantage of this new mode of transport to bring in their barley malt and coal for raising steam.

The two major brewers, Bass and Allsopps, were both located near the railway and as the town prospered and grew, it encouraged many of smaller breweries to be built further out. All required maltings, cooperages and bottling facilities and transport for the

raw materials, which resulted in quickly expanding private railway networks to connect the different departments to their brewhouses.

The MR was quickly followed into Burton by the London North Western Railway (LNWR) and the North Staffordshire Railway (NSR), all wanting to cash in on these potentially lucrative phenomena. Numerous branch

This splendid photo is the Bass Brewery equivalent to London and South Western Railway's Dugald Drummond's personal inspection and visitor saloon, named 'The Bug'. This photo shows a well turned out 0-4-0ST No.10 built by Neilson Reid in 1901, works No. 5907 and painted in Midland Red with their VIP/inspection coach behind. The loco was withdrawn from service in 1964 and put on display in the National Brewery Visitor Centre in Burton. The Visitors coach was sold on in 1963.

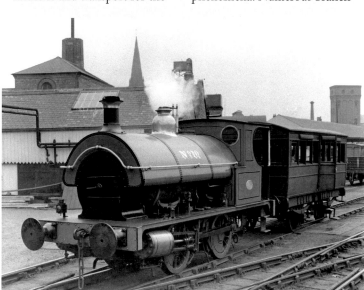

lines and private sidings were constructed and had to cross over public roads in the town where there were 24 gated level crossings and signal boxes for the many semaphore signals. The MR built its engine sheds opposite the Leicester Junction to the west of the town and the LNWR on the Derby side of town with the Wetmore Sidings and Dixie Sidings on both sides of the MR main line that dealt with assembly of hundreds of wagons and despatch of brewery traffic.

The MR was the dominant company and built branch lines around the town such as Bond End and Guild Street Branches with numerous private sidings that served the breweries and their various facilities. One of the major products of brewing beer is a surplus of yeast which was supplied to the 'like it or hate it' Marmite factory near the Branson Sidings by Leicester Junction.

Allsopps was the first brewery to take delivery of a steam engine in 1862, followed a year later by Bass with a 0-4-0 tank engine built locally by Burton's own engine builder, Thornewill and Warham, now still in business as Briggs. In total, Bass had 28 locos in MR red and Allsopps had nine in dark green. Ind Coope had 11 locos painted Brunswick Green and Worthington had 16 locos painted a dark blue as were Marston's five locos.

Burton brewery had four locos, the company being acquired by Ind Coope. Salts had four locos painted in a brownish maroon and Charrington's had only two locos, both coming under the wing of Bass. Marston, Thompson and Evershed (all former independent companies) had five navy blue locos. Truman, Hanbury and Buxton, another London brewer, had five locos in a mid-green livery. Bass had some 20 miles (32km) of private sidings that kept at least 12 engines on duty at any one time and they had a private coach for taking visitors around their network.

Private wagons were owned by several

A busy day at one of the Burton sidings with a rake of open and covered wagons ready to leave with its cargo of beer! The crew are chatting to the shunter leaning on his pole. The locomotive is a Midland Railway 2-6-0, No. 42743 built in 1927, works No. 5755. It was withdrawn from service in 1964. This type of locomotive was called a Crab, possibly because of the shape of the outside cylinders and valves the resembled crab claws!

This view at Allsopps Crossing signal box in 1953, which controls the line crossing from Allsopps Cooperage to 'New Brewery' immediately behind the locomotive. The locomotive is standing on the Guild Street Branch between MR main line and Allsopps 'old brewery' on the Hay Branch beside the River Trent. Locomotive No. 12 is an 0-4-0ST in the Bass/Worthington fleet, built by Hudswell Clarke in 1896 and sold on in 1958. Note the old bar signal set to stop traffic crossing the Guild Street Branch.

major brewers in Burton including Bass, Worthington, Ind Coope, Allsopps and Truman. The latter two both used bulk tank wagons for dispatch to regional brewers for bottling, especially Allsopps with its early lager beer. Internal user wood wagons were once common place around Burton, with Bass and Worthington sending out their products in elaborately signed covered vans. The bulk of inward traffic was coal in the collieries' own rolling stock, and barley and malt largely coming from the many maltings in East Anglia. Wagons of the main line companies were also much used.

High volumes of coal and coke were required at each location around the town for steam boilers, especially where there were water wells, most

This photo of the 1950s shows the old LNWR engine shed and water tower on the left. The Saunder's Branch is off the photo to the extreme left and in the middle distance are the Allsopps maltings. An ex-LMS Fowler 0-6-0, Class 4F waits to take out its next train of beer and in the foreground a Class 08 shunter is busy putting together the next train. There are two shunters with their poles in attendance. Note the gas lamp and shunting signals.

The undercroft or basement of St Pancras station in London was where a great deal of beer from Burton was unloaded and temporarily stored. A wagon hoist between platforms 4 and 5 lowered them down into the undercroft where the 18 gallon (82 litre) casks and metal crates of bottled beer were unloaded. Wagons could be manoeuvred by using wagon turntables. Brewer's drays could then access the area to remove their beer. Since the rebuild of St Pancras this large area has been transformed into the departure lounge for Eurostar services to the Continent.

necessary for maltings where the barley had to be constantly wetted. The four major brewers between them had 40 miles of private railway tracks which despatched 400,000 wagons from Burton each year in their heyday. Today there is virtually nothing left of the railway network, but Burton is a town of beer and for many years stood apart from all other towns as a railway metropolis without any rivals.

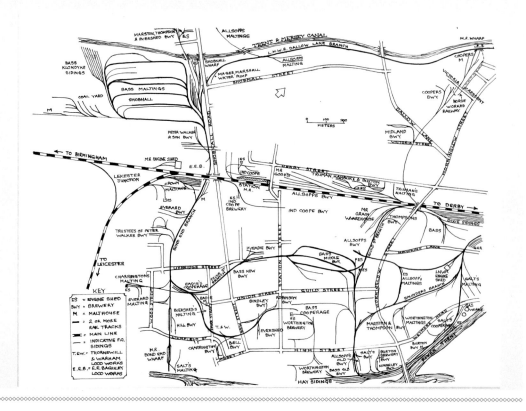

Bodmin and Wadebridge Railway (Wenford Bridge Branch)

At the terminus goods yard in Wenford Bridge, one of the sidings is connected to the standard gauge tramway to the De Lank Quarry Company. A down gradient of 1:8 was achieved using a counterbalanced cable with wagons hauled back to Wenford Bridge by horses but replaced in the 1920s by a Simplex petrol motor. This photo was taken in 1934.

Cornwall is a beautiful county with a rich history of mineral extraction over a long period of time. Among the minerals quarried are copper, chiefly along the coastal areas; slate quarried from the world famous Delabole quarry; granite from the De Lank quarry and china clay mainly from the St Austell area. China of Par with supplies of the raw material coming from several inland pits, all moved by rail.

This mineral-only branch line catered for two minerals that were derived from one geological feature, granite. This was the Bodmin to Wenford Bridge single track line which made connection with the former GWR

Bodmin was the first locomotive on the line and was built by Fletcher Jennings of Whitehaven in 1863. It was an 0-4-0T locomotive and entered service in 1864 and stayed in service until 1896 when it was sold for scrap by the LSWR.

Built by Manning Wardle in 1862 this 0-6-0ST named *Jumbo* entered service on the railway in 1885 to 1895 when LSWR sent it to be scrapped at Nine Elms after 32 years' service.

line at Bodmin, and later (1895), as part of the London & South Western Railway (L&SWR) network at Wadebridge giving access to Padstow to the west and Exeter and London to the east. Thus it became the Bodmin and Wadebridge Railway. Ownership finally passed to Southern Railway on January 1, 1923 at the Big Four grouping.

The branch was opened in 1834 to the standard gauge and ran through the wooded valley of the river Camel to Wenford Bridge.

The original track was 42lb laid on granite setts with two holes drilled to each for retaining rail bolts with a total line length of 12 miles 38 chains (19.8 km). There were four ungated road crossings.

The branch carried freight in both directions with sea sand loaded from the riverside sand dock in Wadebridge for agricultural use, plus coal for the scattered communities inland from Bodmin. On the return journey grey quality granite was

The remains of the Wenford Bridge clay 'dries' slowly being taken over by nature, but the loading bank is still visible where the dried clay was loaded into the empty standard gauge wagons. The chimney is from the boiler that heats and dries the clay.

A specially adapted china clay wagon in Bodmin General Station yard during 2010. It is an open wagon with a raised rail across its length for a weatherproof covering in the shape of a tent. The diagonal metal strips at the end of each side of the wagon indicate the side openings.

transported from Wenford Bridge to Bodmin for onward transfer by rail. At Wenford Bridge, a privately owned standard gauge tramway branched off a siding at the terminus goods yard, and after crossing over a minor road commenced a gradient of 1:8 for half a mile (0.8km) on a rope balanced incline. The tramway then continued for a mile (1.6 km) to the De Lank Granite Quarry, which at its peak covered 54 acres.

The granite quarry had several sidings to stone dressing sheds and loading up platforms. The tramway was laid in 1880 and later as business increased, a Simplex petrol engine locomotive was acquired for shunting at the several quarry sidings. The high quality granite was used to build several of London's river bridges.

The end of the line at Wenford Bridge in September 1952 with a Beattie 2-4-0WT No. 30585, built in 1874 by Beyer Peacock, shunting some wagons for its return journey back to Wadebridge. Some china clay wagons are in the siding to the left. This locomotive was allocated to Wadebridge Shed (72F) from the beginning and was withdrawn from there in December 1962.

This 1927 photo shows wagons being loaded with the dry clay from the dries. In front is a Beattie 2-4-0WT No. 0314 (LSWR) built in 1874 with stove pipe chimney that started operations from Wadebridge in the 1890s and was finally withdrawn in December 1962. On Nationalisation of the railways to BR its number became 30585.

China clay traffic from Wenford Bridge commenced in 1862 with clay from workings on Stannon Moor, some six miles (9.6km) from Wenford Bridge yard, and was piped the full distance to Clay Dries at Wenford Bridge, alongside the yard sidings. The founding company was the Stannon China Clay Company which was acquired by the English China Clay Company in 1919. This important export company today operates in Cornwall as Imerys Minerals

from a modern installation on the river Fowey with trains running regularly via Lostwithiel alongside the Fowey River.

Early in the 20th century the Clay Dries and other processing buildings were extended alongside the loop sidings at Wenford Bridge. The china clay process began with the arrival of the clay slurry from the inland pits pumped into settling tanks with water being drained off. The clay slurry was then pumped into tanks and screened to remove

This was a view in 2010 across the A389 Bodmin to Wadebridge road looking in the direction of Dunmere Halt Junction where the standard gauge single track can be seen embedded in the tarmac. Behind is Dunmere siding formerly known as Borough Bounds Wharf where the line then continued to Wenford Bridge. Dunmere Halt station is just 200yds up the main road to the left, where the line ran under the main road.

Dunmere Halt was the first station after Dunmere Halt Junction on the short 1.6 mile (2.56km) branch to Bodmin North station. The line to Wenford Bridge branched away at Dunmere Halt Junction. The road bridge carries the A389 Bodmin to Wadebridge main road.

any impurities. Next, the clay was pressed and passed onward to rotary driers with the process taking around 40 minutes. The drying process reduced moisture to around 10%, and the clay was then tipped into 'Linhays' for storage and eventual loading onto open railway wagons. The wagons were covered with overhead sheeting and designated as 'Clay Hoods'. These then became 'white' wagons because of the cleansed clay contents. Production in the earlier years was 1,680 tons per week, rising to 2,100 tons with improved equipment and 30 employed staff.

Services started in on the line in 1864 and included two 0-4-0T locomotives built by Fletcher Jennings & Co. of Whitehaven. The first to arrive was *Bodmin* built in 1863, followed shortly after by *Scot*. Others that followed were *Camel* and *Elephant*, both 0-6-0 tender locomotives built by Neath Abbey Iron Works in

Bodmin General is now the home of the preserved Bodmin and Wenford Railway and a Swindon built GWR Class 4200, 2-8-0T No. 37142 pulls into the platform with a train on a rather wet Saturday afternoon in 2010. The Locomotive entered service in March 1916 and was withdrawn from BR service in April 1964 and has now has been beautifully restored to provide many more years of service.

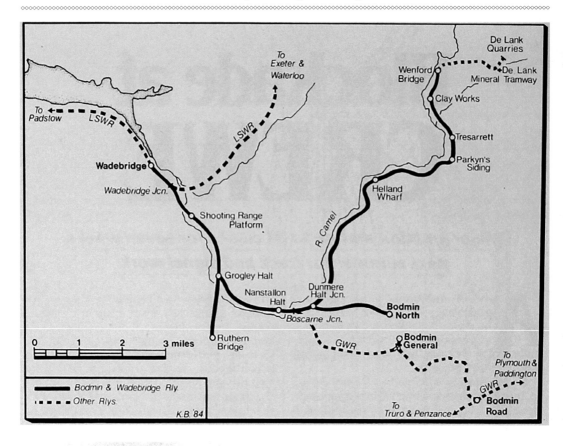

Bodmin and Wadebridge
Railway in Cornwall
with one of three special
locomotives, 2-4-0 tank
used on the mineral line to
Wenford bridge and the clay
works and granite quarry.

September 1834 and 1836 respectively. London & South Western Railway (L&SWR) provided *Jumbo*, a Manning Wardle 0-6-0ST built in 1862 and entered service on the line in 1885 until 1895. It was then scrapped at Nine Elms. Wagons and coaches, such as they were, were made and repaired locally in the company's own workshop.

The next important milestone on the railway was the need for the right locomotive to make light of the heavy minerals that were carried in each direction and to easily navigate the sharp curves of the Wenford Bridge branch. In 1895 the L&SWR transferred three 2-4-0WT Class 0298, Beattie Well tank locomotives to Wadebridge, numbers 298, 314 and 329, via their own network. All three were built by Beyer Peacock between 1874 and 1875. Originally they each had a stovepipe chimney, but were reduced in height when Drummond

boilers replaced the existing ones in the 1930s.

During the British Rail days an assortment of locomotives were frequently seen on the Bodmin and Wadebridge, especially L&SWR Adams 0-4-4T Class 02 and the Beattie Well Tanks.

The quarry tramway was closed on October 31, 1966. The Beeching Plan closed the Wadebridge to Bodmin line in January 1967 although some freight continued to use Wadebridge yard until 1978. Clay continued to be carried down the Wenford Bridge branch until September 1983 when a Class 08 diesel shunter brought the last load of clay from the dries.

Today the familiar sounds of locomotives have gone and the track has been removed and the line has become the Camel Trail for walkers to enjoy the scenery through this attractive valley.

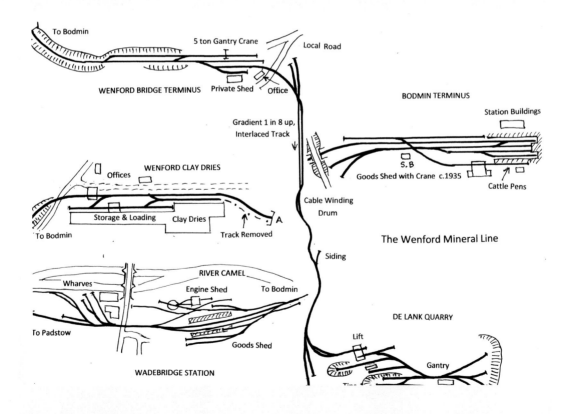

Bowaters & Sittingbourne & Kemsley Light Railway

This shows Brazil Class 0-4-2ST *Premier* built in 1905 by Kerr Stuart at the Sittingbourne exchange sidings with the straw conveyor overhead in 1954. This is now the site of the SKLR Viaduct station.

Bowaters Paper Mills

The manufacture of paper in Sittingbourne goes back to around 1877 when Edward Lloyd, a publisher of newspapers and books, purchased Smith's Old Mill to satisfy his company's demand for paper. Raw materials and finished paper were transported to and from the mill and shipping wharf by a horse-drawn tramway, which also had access to the South Eastern and Chatham Railway that brought in china clay, an essential raw material for making paper.

After Edward Lloyd's death in 1890, his son Edward took over the business (Edward Lloyd Ltd). The raw materials were supplied to

A Bagnall 0-6-2T locomotive, *Conqueror*, built in 1922 at Ridham dock waiting to be loaded with its next assignment around the complex in 1954.

This is a Bagnall, Baretto Class 0-6-2T built in 1932 and named *Alpha*. It is seen here in 1954 approaching the incinerator loop.

the mill by barges that sailed up Milton Creek to their wharves. Milton Creek was several miles from the Swale, a narrow stretch of sea water that separates the mainland and the Isle of Sheppey. In 1907 two steam locomotives were introduced on a 2ft 6in (762mm) gauge track to replace the horse drawn wagons that took the raw materials from the wharf to the mill. These were Kerr Stuart Brazil Class 0-4-

2ST locomotives named *Premier* and *Leader* and with the addition of *Excelsior* in 1908.

By 1913 Sittingbourne Paper Mill was the largest producer of newsprint in the world with 17 machines making over 2000 tonnes of paper every week and supplied the needs of London's Fleet Street. By this time Milton Creek was silting up and Ridham deep-water dock was constructed on the Swale for sea-going ships

This locomotive is probably *Conqueror* with paper loaded on three flatbed wagons at Ridham dock in the early 1960s.

Jubilee was one of the standard gauge locomotives. It was a 0-4-0ST No. 2542 built by Bagnall in 1936 especially for Edward Lloyd of Bowaters in 1936. It is on the line to Swale Halt and to the left is the rail/road lift bridge over the Swale.

The second standard gauge locomotive was an ex South Eastern and Chatham Railway (SECR) P Class 0-6-0T locomotive No. 31178 built at Ashford Works in 1910 and named *Pioneer 2* (*Jubilee* was No.1). It was withdrawn from BR service in 1958 and purchased by Bowaters in 1959 and seen here in September 1964. It is now in preservation on the Bluebell Railway.

to dock, off-load the raw material and reload with the finished paper products. In 1914 at the start of the First World War the Admiralty had taken over the dock and extended the railway to connect with Ridham Dock.

After the war, the railway and dock were returned to Bowaters and they opened another paper mill at Kemsley Down in 1924,

which was about halfway between Sittingbourne and Ridham Dock, ending up with 10 miles (16km) of track. Apart from the narrow gauge railway there was a standard gauge system that ran around Kemsley and Ridham Dock and connected to the Sittingbourne to Sheerness branch of the national network.

It wasn't until 1936 that the

This is *Melior* an 0-4-0ST built in 1924 by Kerr Stuart. The photo was taken over the May Bank Holiday in 2011 and trains were boarded at Milton Regis (Asda) Halt as vandalism at Sittingbourne Viaduct station rendered the station unusable for passengers at that time.

Bowater family purchased the company and it became the Bowater Lloyd Group, usually just called Bowaters.

In 1969 the narrow gauge railway was deemed slow and old fashioned, but had provided a good industrial service over the years. It also ran a scheduled service for the employees with seven station stops from Sittingbourne to the mills, but was sadly closed down and handed over to the new lessees, the Locomotive Club of Great Britain who formed the Sittingbourne and Kemsley Light Railway. In fact, this was the last industrial narrow gauge railway operating in Britain.

Melior arriving at Kemsley Down station in reverse with a short train in 2011.

The locomotives operating the Bowater's network were;

1905	Kerr Stuart	Brazil Class	0-4-2ST	Premier
1905	Kerr Stuart	Brazil Class	0-4-2ST	Leader
1908	Kerr Stuart	Brazil Class	0-4-2ST	Excelsior
1920	Kerr Stuart	Baretto Class	0-6-2T	Superior
1921	English Electric Battery		0-4-0	The Tank (known as)
1922	Bagnall		0-6-2T	Conqueror
1924	Bagnall	Fireless	2-4-0F	Unique
1924	Kerr Stuart	Brazil Class	0-4-2ST	Melior
1929	Bagnall	Fireless	0-4-0F	Victor
1932	Bagnall	Baretto Class	0-6-2T	Alpha
1934	Bagnall	Baretto Class	0-6-2T	Triumph
1940	Bagnall	Baretto Class	0-6-2T	Superb
1950	Manning Wardle		0-6-2T	Chevallier (2nd hand)
1953	Bagnall		0-4-4-0T	Monarch (articulated)
1953	Hunslet	4wDM		Not named

There were also two locomotives that worked the standard gauge network;

1959   SECR P Class(31178) 0-6-0T *Pioneer 2* (built Ashford 1910)
Withdrawn from BR in 1958 and purchased by Bowaters in 1959. Now preserved on the Bluebell Railway.
1936 Bagnall No.2542 0-4-0ST *Jubilee*
It was built for Edward Lloyd (Bowaters) in 1936 and in 1976 went to East Anglia Railway Museum to be completely restored.

This photo was taken at the Sittingbourne Viaduct station in June 2008 with *Triumph* a Bagnall, Baretto Class 0-6-2T built in 1934 inching its way into the platform with its red and cream coaches.

The sad scene shows *Unique*, the narrow gauge 2-4-0F fireless locomotive built by Bagnall in 1924 in amongst nature at Kemsley Down station in 2011.

Sittingbourne & Kemsley Light Railway (S&KLR).

Since becoming a narrow gauge heritage line it has endured a somewhat chequered existence bearing in mind that the line ran through industrial territory. In 1970 the line from Kemsley Down to Ridham Dock was abandoned to make way for redevelopment of the mills and in 2008 survived total closure due to the owners closing Sittingbourne Mill in 2007 and selling the land that the railway leased.

However, the railway was saved but remained closed to the public until October 2010 when a short period of service between Milton Regis Halt and Kemsley Down enabled its passengers to celebrate its 40 years as a heritage railway. Maintenance problems at Sittingbourne Viaduct and station prevented a full reopening to the public until May 27, 2012. S&KLR has a good variety of ex Bowaters locos, rolling stock and others.

The Bowaters steam locos are;
Alpha (cosmetic restoration), *Leader*, *Melior*, *Premier* (under restoration), *Superb*, *Triumph* (expiry of boiler cert.), *Unique* (static display).
Other locos are;

Hudson Hunslet	4wDM	4182	*Victor* built 1953
Ruston & Hornsby	0-4-0DM	435403	*Edward Lloyd* built 1961
Hunslet	4xDH	6651	*Barton Hall* built 1965
Andrew Barclay	0-4-0F	1876	*No. 1* built 1925

This is a SG loco from Bowaters Northfleet and on static display.

Peckett & Sons	0-4-0ST	614	No.3 Bear built 1896

This loco on static display is the oldest surviving SG Peckett.

A lovely sunny afternoon on August 1, 2020 shows *Melior* steaming along the viaduct at Milton Regis with its train of red and cream coaches. The driver and fireman obviously enjoying the trip after the first coronavirus 'lockdown' was relaxed.

The S&KLR coaching stock consists of a selection of 12 open and closed coaches in various stages of operational usage. Some are ex Bowaters (they were used to provide 24-hour passenger services for the employees). Four were from the Chattenden and Upnor Railway. The freight stock is quite numerous and varied with steel and wooden pulp wagons, flat wagons and hoppers.

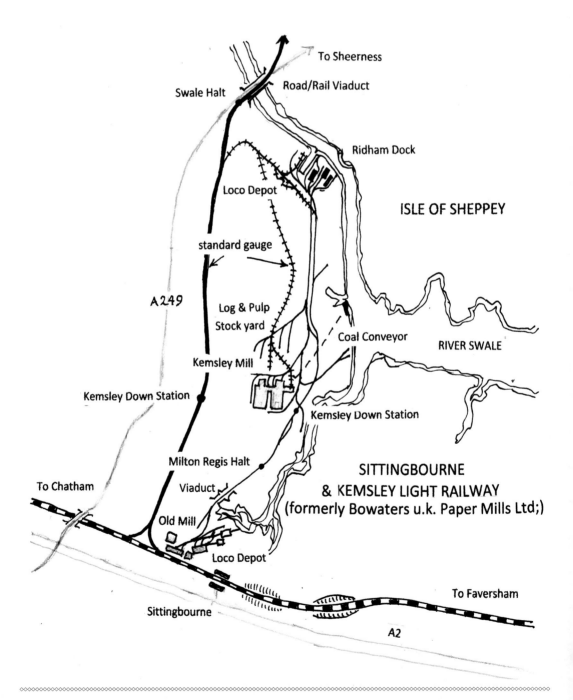

Dove Holes and Tunstead are two very large limestone quarries operated by Cemex and Tarmac respectively that are located between the Dove Holes rail tunnel and Great Rocks Dale in Derbyshire's Peak district.

Before looking more closely at these

THE MIDLAND RAILWAY

A view in 2015 from the over-bridge at Peak Forest looking north with the up and down goods lines on the left. A rake of EWS empty aggregate wagons have arrived ready to be shunted into the reception sidings. The conveyor system for loading into empty wagons can be seen connecting into the loading shed with an almost loaded train gradually edging forwards behind a Class 66 No. 66050. The wagons are ex HTA coal hopper wagons converted for aggregate use.

quarries and their connection to the national rail network it is essential to mention a little of the historic background regarding the Midland Railway (MR) route that connected Derby to Manchester across the Peak District's spectacular and beautiful limestone hills and through its rocky valleys.

Back in the heady days of 'railway mania' in the 1840s, competition between the railway companies often turned into hatred; to think that a rival company could reach a destination that another

company had not yet managed to achieve was considered a major achievement. Sometimes the end result was two lines almost running parallel to each other with two terminal stations side by side!

As so many small railway companies sprung up around the UK, it was realised that longer distance rail travel could be achieved by the larger companies coming to suitable running arrangements by connecting into the lines of smaller ones to reach the chosen destination. These arrangements benefitted both

An EWS Class 66 No. 66620 heads up a train of fully loaded mixed aggregate wagons including some HOA and similar hopper wagons during 2014. A freightliner Class 66 trundles along the down line. A blue, ex RMC Roadstone, 0-6-0 Sentinel, No. 10107, built in 1963 sits in the head shunt siding.

passenger and freight services; and so it was the case between two major companies, the Midland Railway and the London and North Western Railway (LNWR) who were constantly battling against each other. The destination prize for these two was Manchester's London Road Station from Midland's prestigious St Pancras station and LNWR's Euston station in the quickest time and the shortest route possible.

The MR route from Derby took it north on the Leeds line then branched left at Ambergate Junction (commenced Sept 1860) going northwest through Cromford, Matlock, Rowsley and Bakewell with the gradient increasing to 1 in 100, as the locomotives steamed through tunnels and over viaducts, especially the spectacular Monsal Viaduct. The line then entered Miller's Dale station consisting of two platforms plus a bay for the Buxton Branch. At Buxton

Looking south from Peak Forest over-bridge a Class 66 pulls its loaded aggregate train along the down goods line to a point where it can stop, run round and take the train across to the up goods line going north through Dove Holes Tunnel. Two DB Schenker Class 66s of unknown number sit idling in sidings together with a DB Schenker Class 60 No. 60044. Photo was taken in 2015.

A Class 60, No. 60044 idling, waiting for signal clearance at Peak Forest. The wagon is for transporting steel strip and was built by Thrall Europa at their York works. A total of 310 were built between 1998 and 1999. They have telescopic rounded hoods made of corrugated steel and are affectionately known as 'Nissen Huts'! (2017)

the Midland built a fine station (1867) for this spa town only to be copied by the LNWR who built a similar one next to it for its own service.

Leaving Miller's Dale station the MR main line turned north, away from the Buxton branch, on an upward incline through Great Rocks Dale and Peak Forest station to Dove Holes tunnel 2,984yds (2,729m) long, which was the summit of the line at 980ft (298m). The tunnel was only 183ft (56m) below the L&NWR line and keeping it open for traffic was a constant problem with the ingress of water and collapses. The line then continued to Chinley, Chapel-en-le-Frith, through Disley Tunnel, Hazel Grove and into Manchester. The line was fully operational in 1867.

The Midland eventually took over the smaller rail companies whose lines it used to achieve its route to Manchester. During 1923, when the various railway companies were placed in their Big Four groups, the MR and LNWR became part of London Midland and Scottish Railways (LMS) and competition had to stop and some rationalisation started to take place – although nothing really changed on the Peak District lines as they were almost wholly Midland Railway.

As a result of the Beeching Report of 1962 the Peak Line was under threat of closure, especially to passengers, and stations from Rowsley to Miller's Dale were swiftly closed along with the Buxton branch, although freight trains carrying stone from the quarries continued along that branch. The last direct St Pancras to Manchester express service, in 1968, was diverted away from the Peak Line and all unnecessary track was then lifted.

Today, the lime stone quarries continue to thrive and the line serving Tunstead and Dove Holes is now known as the Great Rocks Line. The disused Peak Forest station that closed in 1967 is now used as part of the support function for the Dove Holes quarry and is situated just below the overbridge in the village of Peak Dale. The 1923 Great Rocks Junction, 34 lever, signal box is still operational at the end of the double track from the north to control Tunstead quarry traffic. Continuing the short distance south towards Buxton the line is single track and there are plenty of original semaphore signals on the Great Rocks Line to admire.

A selection of aggregate wagons seen at Dove Holes in 2014. The two orange coloured wagons are ex RMC Roadstone type JGA and the two at the right are Cemex HOA hopper wagons.

Dove Holes Quarry

Dove Holes Quarry is the largest within the Cemex group and employs around 150 staff and extracts very pure carboniferous limestone. The quarry has been in existence since the early 1900s and was privately owned by a company called Taylor Frith. RMC (Ready Mixed Concrete) bought the quarry in 1983 and they subsequently became a part of Cemex. At the time of writing, the quarry is extracting around four million tonnes of aggregate per year which goes through primary and secondary crushing and washing stages to produce the sizes of aggregate required by the customer.

The aggregate is transported out to customers by road and rail. Around 45% is transported to customers by Cemex's own haulage trucks, but the company prefers to limit deliveries to a 60km (37mile) radius, or customers collect direct and 55% is transported by rail from Cemex's own rail-head situated

To commemorate the contract between Cemex and GB Railfreight in 2020, to regularly transport a high volume of aggregate products to the south to support the building boom, a Class 66 locomotive No. 66780 has been appropriately liveried in Cemex colours displaying both names along the side. The locomotive is named *The Cemex Express* and recycled coal hopper wagons have been made operational for this exercise.

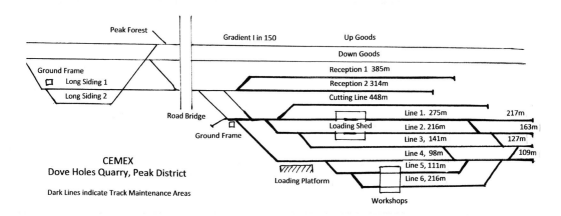

alongside the through line at Peak Dale to its rail depots including Crawley, Bletchley, Ely, Manchester, Selby, Washwood Heath, Norwich, Leeds and Sheffield.

The Cemex rail-head consists of nine sidings including two reception sidings for returning wagons and a cutting line. The other six are joined together to form a series of loop sidings including lines 1 & 2 that run under the Loading Shed being fed from the top by a conveyor system from the quarry area.

Cemex has a mix of bottom discharging hopper wagons and box wagons. GB Railfreight (GBRf) has the contract for the hopper traffic and DB Cargo for the box wagons. A third but important task is to run the shunting operations within the yard to ensure that all wagons are assembled and ready to leave Dove Holes on schedule. This is contracted to Victa Rail Freight.

During June of 2020 it was announced that GBRf had been contracted by Cemex to move a high volume of bulk building materials, namely aggregate for readymix and asphalt plants, from Dove Holes to Crawley for the building boom in and around London and the Southeast. To accomplish this task a number of ex coal hoppers have been brought back to an operational standard. The consist is a rake of 22 to 26 wagons and is operated once a week. A GBRf Class 66 locomotive No. 66780, newly liveried in blue and white, was named *The Cemex Express* at a ceremony held at Dove

Holes. Unfortunately, all rail traffic going to the south has to take the northern route through Dove Holes tunnel then swing round towards Sheffield before coming south.

Tunstead Quarry

About three quarters of a mile (1.2km) south of Dove Holes the Great Rocks Line gives access to Tunstead Quarry, one of Europe's largest quarries operated by Tarmac. Like Dove Holes it produces millions (six) of tons of limestone products of which around 50% is transported away by rail.

Looking back, there were many small quarries in the vicinity of the Midland Railway line and in 1891 Buxton Lime Firms Ltd (BLF) was formed from 13 of these quarries and opened a new quarry known as South Works with Brunner & Mond as their primary customer. The crushed limestone was used in their manufacture of soda-ash, sodium bicarbonate, calcium chloride and soap. Brunner & Mond then purchased a controlling interest in BLF in 1918 and by 1927 had merged with others to become Imperial Chemical Industries (ICI), the largest chemical company in the world.

As demand for limestone products increased, so quarry reserve areas were opened up; rail traffic increased and the rail-head was continually in a state of change to shunt

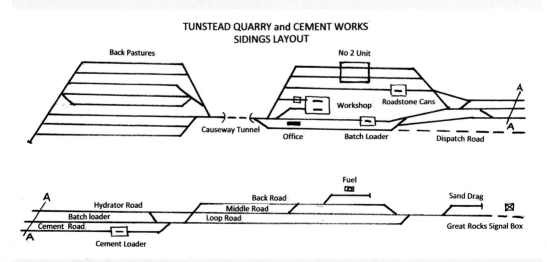

TUNSTEAD QUARRY and CEMENT WORKS
SIDINGS LAYOUT

Right: Two Class 37 diesels tackling the gradient of 1 in 50 with a fully loaded train of bogie hopper wagons loaded with limestone, approaching the long Dove Holes tunnel, Peak District.

Above: The colourful orange livery bogie hopper wagons of the RMC company who worked the limestone quarries at Dove Holes, Peak District with a train hauled by Class 8F, 2-8-0, working hard on the stiff grades.

This is Tunstead Quarry during 1935 and clearly shows the well organised 610mm (2ft) narrow gauge network with the main access tracks in the foreground and the numerous angled spurs going to the quarry face. At the end of each spur is a 'Jubilee' side tipping wagon to receive the aggregate as it is quarried. These wagons are then collected and shunted into trains by four-wheeled Simplex petrol/ diesel locomotives. The standard gauge line can be seen at the foot of the rock face on the extreme left.

and manage the wagons. In March 2013 another change of ownership placed the business in the hands of the Lafarge Tarmac group of which Lafarge (France) is the biggest manufacturer of cement.

A new plant was built in 2004 to increase manufacture of cement at Tunstead. To transport this high volume of cement, Tarmac acquired 23 bogie tank wagons, liveried in white with 'Buxton Lime and Cement', with the strap line of 'using rail to cut emissions' in green letters and the Climate Change symbol with generous green and yellow broad bands at one end; these are coded JGAs. The JPA wagons were built by Feldbinder of Germany in 2008 in aluminium, with a total of 26 with

An example of
a 2ft (610mm)
gauge Motor
Rail (Simplex)
locomotive used to
haul the 'Jubilee'
wagons from the
rock face. This one
numbered RS/34
is probably a 20hp
diesel, 20/36 built
around 1930
and developed
21bhp at 800rpm
and 36bhp
at 1,500rpm.
Originally based
in Lewes, East
Sussex, the
company moved
to Bedford in
1916 and built
many similar
locomotives,
including
armoured
locomotives for the
War Department
during the First
World War.
There are many in
preservation.

a capacity of 101.6 tonnes. Thirty of the French JGA steel cement tank wagons were built in 2003.

Tunstead Quarry has seen a variety of locomotive traction over the years. In the 1930s a 2ft 0in (610mm) gauge system was in use, regularly changing its spider web of sidings to the quarry working faces using 1932 built Simplex, four-wheeled petrol/diesel locomotives to shunt and haul the small 'jubilee' side tipping wagons.

Moving on, a number of

A Freightliner
Class 66 with a
train of cement
tanker wagons
having been
through the
cement loading
shed gradually
pulls away towards
the Great Rocks
signal box before
joining the main
goods line, seen
here on the left
emerging from the
tunnel.

locomotives have been used on-site over the years;
1. Ruston Hornsby   0-4-0 DE   built 1957, named   *Trevithick,*
        rebuilt by ICI at Tunstead. Out of use in 1976 .
2. Ruston Hornsby   0-6-0   built in 1950, rebuilt by ICI at Tunstead.
3. Yorkshire Engine,   0-4-0 DE   built 1956,   *Wallace Akers.*
4. Rolls-Royce   0-6-0 DE   built 1969, rebuilt 1974 by Thomas Hill.
5. Sentinel   4w   built 1960   *Nidderdale.*
6. Yorkshire Engine   0-4-0 DE   built 1956,   *Davy.*
7. Thomas Hill,   4w DH   built 1979.
8. Thomas Hill   4w DH   built 1980.   *Harry Townley.*
9. Thomas Hill   0-6-0   built 1969,   *Dovedale,*
        rebuilt by Thomas Hill in 1986.
10. Hunslet   0-6-0   built 2015,   *Patrick D. Duggan,*
        owned and serviced by Hunslet.
11. Hunslet   0-6-0   built 2015,   *Graham Lee JNR,*
        owned and serviced by Hunslet.
12. Vollert DR 3000, Co Co, 650hp, shunting robot for cement loading only.

The Midland Railway's Great Rocks Line runs at the bottom of a very deep cutting and a large amount of limestone has been removed from the cliff sides to accommodate the 5¾ miles (9.2km) of quarry sidings and five loading terminals where loading is mainly accomplished using conveyor systems. There are also 'wall loading' sidings where mechanical shovels load aggregate into the waiting wagons. Freightliner has a contract to move limestone products to its facility at Garston, Liverpool and has a crew depot on site at Tunstead. DB Cargo has contracts to deliver a range of products including roadstone and crushed limestone for construction work around London and the southeast.

In 1997 Cemex and Tarmac put competition aside, created Buxton Rail, and secured a joint contract to supply 1.4 million tonnes of aggregate from their Dove Holes and Tunstead quarries to build Manchester Airport.

With the tremendous amount of aggregate freight going south there is a move to reopen the old Midland line through the Peak District back towards Derby, Leicester and on to London offering a quicker and more direct route to the south. What goes around, comes around!

Before joining the main goods line from the quarry, trains require the clear signal from the Great Rocks signal box. These shunting signals are lower quadrant Midland Railway type; one set for the quarry line and one for the up goods line.

Having passed the clear signal the train of 15 cement tankers with Freightliner Class 66 No. 66620 at the front, slowly moves onto the goods up line (north) and passed the Great Rocks signal box. The signal box is a Midland Railway Type 4D fitted with a 34 lever tappet frame and was opened on March 11, 1923 by the London, Midland and Scottish Railway and replaced an existing box of 1891.

Some JGA Buxted Lime & Cement (Tarmac) bogie cement hopper wagons made by Arbel Fauvet in France during 2003 and leased from VTG. In the background is the German shunting robot, Vollert DR300, built in 2002 and developing 650bhp, which is owned and serviced by Tarmac. Seen here receiving some service.

A good side view of an Arbel Fauvet JGA cement hopper wagon. This one is number VTG 11721 and has two twin axle bogies and discharges its load from the bottom of the tank. It can hold 69,727 Litres of cement and 66.2 tons maximum weight with a tare weight of 23.3 tons (weight without cement). It rightly advertises the fact that using rail rather than road, where possible, certainly cuts harmful emissions.

The cement is loaded into the wagons by a bellows that locates with the two top loading hatches located at each end of the wagon, as each wagon moves through the Cement Loader Shed.

One of the two Hunslet Engine Company's 0-6-0 diesel shunters, *Graham Lee Jnr*, delivered in 2015. It is rated at 475bhp and weighs in at 60 tons. It is seen here shunting cement tankers through the cement loading shed. Graham Lee's company, LH Group, acquired what remained of the Hunslet company in 2005 and was subsequently acquired by the US company WABTEC.

Gloucestershire Warwickshire Steam Railway

A view looking towards Winchcombe station in 1960 with a mixed goods train headed up by a GWR Class 2251, 0-6-0 tender locomotive, built at Swindon Works and was the replacement for the aging 0-6-0 Dean Goods. The number is unknown but 120 were built between 1930 and 1948. Note the angle of the Winchcombe name board.

Ready to leave Toddington station during a dismal December afternoon on December 12, 1998 with a Santa Special is *Raveningham Hall*, a GWR modified Hall Class 4-6-0, No. 6960. It was built in March 1944, taken out of service in June 1964 and saved for preservation from Barry scrapyard in 1972. This Santa Special took the short journey to Winchcombe and back with presents for the children and sherry and mince pies for the mums and dads.

This volunteer-run, standard gauge, heritage railway operates along the border of the Cotswolds between the two counties and like most heritage lines there is always a back story.

Originally the line was part of the Great Western Railway's Cheltenham-Stratford upon-Avon-Birmingham line known as the Honeybourne line, handling passenger and freight traffic. Built between 1901 and 1906, the southern

The now famous *Black Prince* in December 1998 being readied for work in Toddington yard. This BR 2-10-0, No. 92203 was built at Swindon Works in April 1959 and was taken out of BR service in November 1967. It was then purchased from BR by artist David Shepherd and has visited several heritage railways, but was bought by the North Norfolk Railway in 2015 where it currently resides.

section ran north through the attractive Cotswold countryside from Cheltenham to the towns of Bishops Cleave, Winchcombe, Toddington and Broadway to the junction of the Worcester-Oxford Line. There was already a junction from the Worcester-Oxford Line to go north to Stratford-upon-Avon, but was single track, which had to be doubled. The junction was remodelled to allow through trains from Cheltenham to bypass Honeybourne station, which was about half a mile (0.8km) on the Worcester side of the Worcester-Oxford Line by using an underbridge.

Passenger services were originally provided by steam GWR railmotors and then by 0-4-2T auto trains that continued until the late 1950s, but by 1960 there were no through services to

At Toddington station in 2014 a BR Class 117, three-car DMU, Nos. W51360, W59510 & W51363 approaches from the Winchcombe direction. This class of DMU were built by the Pressed Steel Company in Linwood, Scotland between 1959 and 1961. They were gradually replaced and the last to go was from train operating company Silverlink in 2000 when they were replaced by Class 150 Sprinters.

This is a Scammell Scarab, a three-wheeled tractor and trailer, used in great numbers by BR from 1948 onwards until production ceased in 1968. Seen here in 2014, in BR Southern Region green, it shows the Scammell badge surrounding the single headlight. Older readers will certainly remember these three-wheelers with some affection as the holiday trunk was thrown in the back, taken to the local station for onward travel to your holiday station and then delivered to your hotel.

A rural station scene at Toddington in 2014 with the BR Class 117, three-car DMU sitting in platform 1 and a train ready to leave from platform 2 for Winchcombe and Cheltenham Racecourse. The diesel is a Class 47, No. 47376, *Freightliner 1995*, a Brush type 4, built by Brush at Loughborough in 1965. It became a part of the Freightliner fleet in 1995 and became its flagship locomotive.

Stratford and passengers had to change at Honeybourne station. The line did see a mixture of longer haul express trains to West Country resorts, Bristol, Fishguard and Pembroke Dock. Freight services consisted mainly of mixed trains of fruit and veg from the Vale of Evesham, coal for local merchants, iron ore and steel from the steelworks in South Wales. Although most of these trains were steam hauled, the line was no stranger to diesel locomotives with Inter-City Diesel Multiple Units, Hymek, Class 47 and warship classes occasionally seen.

However, as in the case of most minor lines it was gradually run down from the 1960s in favour of the adjacent Midland Line, but remained a relief line until a derailment finally saw its closure in 1977. By 1979 the double track had been lifted for scrap.

During this period some

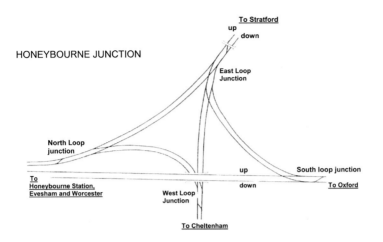

HONEYBOURNE JUNCTION

To Stratford
up
down

East Loop
Junction

North Loop
junction

up

South loop junction

To
Honeybourne Station,
Evesham and Worcester

down

To Oxford

West Loop
Junction

To Cheltenham

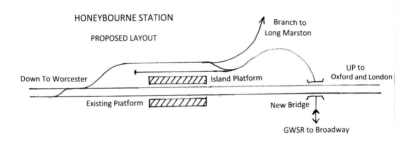

HONEYBOURNE STATION

PROPOSED LAYOUT

Branch to
Long Marston

Down To Worcester

Island Platform

UP to
Oxford and London

Existing Platform

New Bridge

GWSR to Broadway

To Solihull

North Jc.

West Jc.

To Warwick

Hatton

Claverdon

North Jc.

To Henley-in-Arden

West Jc.

Bearley

Wilmcote

Birmingham Rd.

Stratford upon Avon S & M Jc.

Evesham Rd. Crossing H.

Old Town

To Broom

Race Course
Chambers
Crossing H.

Milcote

To Kineton

Long Marston

Pebworth H.

Broad Marston H.

East Jc.

To Worcester

Honeybourne

South Jc.

West Jc.

Weston-sub-Edge

Willersey H.

To Oxford

Broadway

Laverton H.

Toddington

Gretton H.

Gotherington

Hayles
Abbey H.

Winchcombe

Bishop's
Cleeve

Race Course

To Birmingham

Lansdown

High St. H.

Lansdown Jc.

St. James

Malvern Rd.

Cheltenham

To Gloucester

To Kingham

Andoversford

Hatherley Jc.

Gloucester Loop Jc.

To Cirencester

This GWR locomotive, Class 2800, No. 2807 is a 2-8-0 built in 1905 at Swindon Works to haul heavy freight and these locomotives were used extensively over the GWR network. It was withdrawn from service in 1963 and taken to Barry scrapyard and was rescued during 1981 and taken to Toddington yard works. It is owned by Cotswold Steam Preservation Limited.

enthusiasts formed a group to save the railway with the long term view of reopening it from Stratford-upon-Avon to Cheltenham resulting in the Gloucestershire Warwickshire Steam Railway purchasing the trackbed between Broadway and Cheltenham in 1981.

During 1984 a short stretch of line was completed from Toddington with 700yds (640m) of re-laid track and then reaching Winchcombe in 1984 where the line was officially declared open. Over the ensuing years the track was extended, eventually reaching Cheltenham Racecourse in 2003. In the opposite direction work was continuing to reopen the line from Toddington to Broadway with a new station at Broadway which opened at Easter 2018. The longer term aim is to rebuild the six mile (9.6km) line from Broadway to Honeybourne station on the national rail network, currently operated by GWR. Honeybourne station track

layout would change to allow the GWSR line to approach from the south under a bridge carrying the main line and looping around to the island platform on the Up line to Oxford and London. The Long Marston branch would then connect with the both Up and Down lines on the Worcester side. There could also be a connection directly to the GWSR line, but at the time of writing approval for construction of this work had been rejected.

All stations and passing loops on the single track line use lower quadrant semaphore signals operated from four signal boxes with a mixture of Electric Key Token and One Train Staff working depending on operation requirements at the time. The railway is well stocked with both steam and diesel locomotives with the emphasis on GWR steam locomotives. They also have a number of MK1 coach stock. The head office and works are at Toddington.

The Hawkhurst Branch – The Hop Pickers Line

By 1852 both Kent and East Sussex were well connected to London termini with South Eastern's (SER) main line via Redhill, through Tonbridge and Ashford to Folkestone and the branch from Tonbridge through Robertsbridge to Hastings. Both lines then had connections to the Ashford to Hastings line forming a triangular network with nothing within it to service small but important towns such as Horsmonden, Cranbrook, Goudhurst, Hawkhurst and Tenterden.

Colonel Stephens' Kent and East Sussex Railway ultimately ran from Robertsbridge, through Tenterden to Headcorn connecting with the main Folkestone line leaving the other small towns without a railway connection. This area produced a high volume of apples, pears, soft fruit and hops for the brewing

industry and needed better transport.

Various schemes were put forward for a branch line to service the area, but nothing materialised until 1877 when the Cranbrook and Paddock Wood Railway was incorporated to construct a line between the two towns, Paddock Wood being on SER main line to Folkestone. Construction eventually

The original Cranbrook and Paddock Wood Railway Company Crest with a hop flower proudly dominating the centre of the crest.

Opening day for the Paddock Wood to Hope Mill, Goudhurst section of the line. The Cudworth E1 Class 2-4-0 locomotive is seen here splendidly decorated, ready to leave Hope Mill station. The resident engineer, Holman Fred Stephens, who was just 22 years old, was at hand to ensure all went well and no doubt enjoy the accolades.

Horsmonden station with two gentlemen and their dogs posing for the photograph. At that time you were never far away from an oast house seen at the right of the station. The station was built in typical Stephens' style with corrugated sheets and wood with the platform supported by locally quarried stone.

Goudhurst station around the 1940s at the end of the hop picking season with the hop pickers waiting with their baggage, prams, pushchairs and homemade wooden trolleys to catch the hop pickers special back to London Bridge station. This train is double headed by C Class 0-6-0 No. 31717 and D Class 4-4-0 No. 31729. Behind the second locomotive is the baggage wagon with enough room for the luggage.

commenced in 1890 with the 22-year-old Fred Holman Stephens (Colonel) as resident engineer. The line was opened in stages, firstly to Horsmonden and Hope Mill (Goudhurst) on September 12, 1892. The ceremonial train was pulled by a Cudworth E1 Class 2-4-0 No. 112 and draped with garlands of hops and Union flags. The line was then finally extended to its terminus in Hawkhurst with the Grand Opening on September 4, 1893 with all the rejoicing, ceremony and partaking in beer that would be expected and a ceremonial public dinner at the

Queen's Inn. The railway was now part of the South Eastern Railway.

On leaving the bay platform on the up side of Paddock Wood station, the 11.3 mile (18.1km) single track line ran parallel to the main line for about half a mile (0.8km) and then turned to a southerly direction towards Horsmonden, Goudhurst, Cranbrook and terminated at Hawkhurst. Unfortunately, as was the case with so many branch lines, construction costs were a major factor and so any difficult terrain or unnecessary divergence was avoided, and so it was on the Hawkhurst line. Goudhurst

A view of Paddock Wood station looking towards London with a fast coast bound boat train for Dover, on the fast down line headed up by a rebuilt Bulleid Merchant Navy Class 4-6-2 No. 34088 named *213 Squadron*. On the left in the bay platform is the Hawkhurst Line push-pull auto train with a Wainwright SECR H Class 0-4-4T ready to leave with its two coaches. On the far right is the bay platform for the Medway Valley line.

station was 1.5 miles (2.4km) down a steep hill at Hope Mill, with Cranbrook station two miles (3.2km) from the town in the village of Hartley, and Hawkhurst station was in Gills Green one and a half miles (2.4km) from the town.

Hawkhurst station and terminus was built as a through station because it was generally thought at that time that the line may be extended down to meet the Lydd Railway at Appledore and so have access to New Romney and Dungeness, but that dream never materialised.

Hop pickers' trains

The county of Kent has always been known as 'the Garden of England', and not without good cause, as fruit orchards cover vast areas of the lush countryside as once did hop gardens that were the largest industry in the county during Victorian times. Hops are grown on bines that are strung on tall frameworks in long rows and are grown to add a bitter flavour in the production of beer and are harvested around September time. Up until the 1960s harvesting was carried out by hand, a rough and dirty job, but used as a working

A two carriage autotrain at Cranbrook station during September 1951 headed up by an E4 Class 0-6-2T No. 32580. This locomotive was built in Brighton at the SR/BR works in 1903 and was allocated to Tonbridge shed. Note the station master's house that is rather grand for this small branch line.

An H Class 0-4-4T No. 31519 at Hawkhurst station in 1960. This locomotive was built in 1909 at SR Ashford Works and operated from Tonbridge shed (74D) and was withdrawn in 1961. Hawkhurst station is a bit wanting as a terminus as it was originally built as a through station, but the line was never extended beyond the buffer stops.

holiday by the poorer working classes from the east and south of London, who came down to large areas of Kent with their families to pick hops over a three week period. They set up camps and used corrugated or wooden huts or tents to sleep in that were normally supplied by the local farmer. Before being shipped to a brewery, the hops were dried by a fire at the bottom of an oast house, a tall round or square building with a pointed roofs and a cowl on top that was rotated by the wind to aid circulation during the drying process.

To get to their destinations

A typical Kent hop garden scene, circa 1900, the hop garlands are being gathered and the hop kernels picked and placed into the canework baskets. While this is going on the children amuse themselves and help out when encouraged!

This photo shows typical hop pickers huts that would have been supplied by the local farmer at the hop gardens. This particular one is a reconstruction in the station grounds of the Kent and East Sussex Railway at Bodium. Unfortunately, too many years have now passed and virtually all of these temporary dwellings have disappeared.

they boarded 'hop picker specials' from London Bridge Low Level station and the train would drop them off at their prescribed station that was nearest to their hop gardens and perhaps ferried to the farm by the local farmer. Otherwise they just walked! These trains would carry 300-400 hop pickers and there could be up to 25 trains each year. A parcel van was usually next to the locomotive to carry all their bags, boxes and prams!

The hop gardens along the Hawkhurst Line were probably the most prolific in the county and many hop pickers arrived for their annual working holiday, mainly on Sundays when the line was closed to regular traffic. During the hop picking season many other friends and family came down to visit and the local pubs were full to bursting! After the harvest and the mayhem the whole procedure was done in reverse to get everyone back to London.

During the late 1800s there were about 77,000 acres given over to hops in Kent. That had fallen to around 11,000 in 1932 and by the early 1960s machines started being used to harvest the hops. Brewers then began to import hops in pelletized form from China and USA.

Hop pickers were no longer needed but today there are still around 3,000 acres used for growing hops.

Oast houses were all over the hop growing areas of Kent. In this photo the hops have been delivered to the oast house after being picked, then dried and bagged up for delivery to the local brewery.

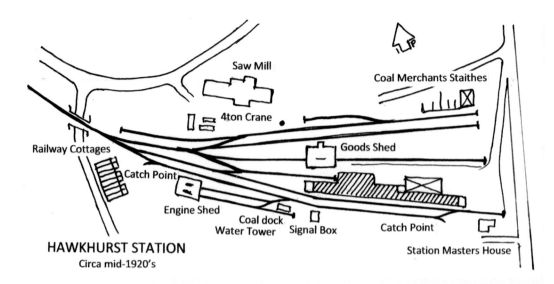

HAWKHURST STATION
Circa mid-1920's

Whoops! During 1948 this train was just leaving Goudhurst station, which had a passing loop, but moved off before the points were switched and ended up along a siding where it hit the buffer stop. The locomotive and first carriage came off the rails and the loco slid down the bank into Percy Henley's hop garden. Fortunately, no one was hurt and the passengers got out for a good look, among them school girls in their macs, hats and satchels made sure they took in the whole scene!

Closure

The announcement of the line's closure did not come as a shock to the local community. It was now 1961 and the hop picking working holidays ceased as mechanical pickers took over the harvesting. Ordinary folks were becoming more affluent and starting to own their own cars and shopping trips to Tunbridge Wells and Maidstone could be made more easily on a Maidstone and District bus than using the trains. Also, goods traffic on this picturesque little line had gradually dwindled away. As Harold Macmillan said in 1957, British people had "never had it so good" as the nation finally seemed to be free of wartime shortages.

This scene of May 2, 1961 was just one month before closure of the line. Taken at Horsmonden station it shows a goods train with a Class C 0-6-0 No. 31592 pulling away from the signal. The loco is ex SECR, built in 1902 and withdrawn in 1967.

This shows a Class 375 EMU entering platform 2 at Paddock Wood station in 2021 leaving the Medway Valley Line from Maidstone West station passing through what used to be large areas of hop gardens with many oast houses, most of which have been converted to domestic use. This platform is the opposite side to what used to be the Hawkhurst bay platform and now part of the car park.

This is Wateringbury station on the Medway Valley line in 2013 looking back towards Paddock Wood. It still had a manual level crossing where the gates were manually opened and closed by the signalman. The station building and station master's house is a very elaborate affair, but the footbridge is a standard SR prefabricated concrete footbridge.

The last day of public service was on Saturday June 10, 1961 when local people turned out to say their farewells to their railway and many enthusiasts with cameras recorded the events in black and white for posterity with a final trip to Hawkhurst.

Rolling stock

For the most part the regular trains in the latter years were connected to operate in push-pull mode with two coaches and probably a Wainwright H Class 0-4-0T where the end carriage had a rear driving compartment and controls that operated the locomotive at the other end. This allowed the train to be pulled to Hawkhurst and pushed back to Paddock Wood, saving time as the locomotive did not have to run round.

In the early days a Cudworth E1 Class 2-4-0 and L Class 2-4-0 Stirling worked the normal passenger services, but during the 1900s Stirling Q Class 0-4-4T locos took on the task. A selection of other classes were used for the 'hop pickers specials' and after the First World War push-pull fittings were introduced to R Class 0-4-4T locomotives and subsequently R and R1 Class and then to the H Class in the 1950s.

Dugald Drummond's renowned 0-6-0 Class 700 of the LSWR/SR working efficiently on its pick-up goods on the Mid Hants branch line in Hampshire.

Other hop garden areas in Kent

Other areas were Canterbury, Faversham, Maidstone and Medway Valley. The 16¼ mile (34km) Medway Valley (MV) line opened in 1896 (SER) and follows the River Medway between Paddock Wood to Maidstone West station and onwards to Strood (Rochester) where it connects with the North Kent line (LCDR) from London Victoria to Dover via Canterbury East.

The MV line, now part of the region's 750V DC 3rd rail system, leaves the bay platform on the down side of Paddock Wood station and veers immediately left in the Maidstone direction. The first station is Beltring, which is about half a mile (0.8km) from the largest complex of oast houses in Kent once owned by the brewing company Whitbreads. Trains to the Medway Valley line left London Bridge and deposited many hop pickers to work in the hop gardens around the immediate area. Today, the station is little used and the Hop Farm, although still with its numerous roundels, is currently privately owned and converted into a family fun and activity centre. The next two stations before Maidstone West are Wateringbury and East Farleigh, which until recently still had manual level crossing gates, but still have their original signal boxes in use.

Mid Hants Railway (Watercress Line)

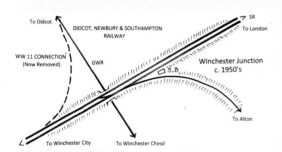

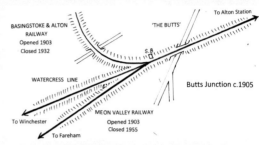

Today, the Mid Hants Railway is affectionately called 'The Watercress Line'. Its back story begins around 1830 when a line was being planned from London to Southampton. After considering many problems, a line was fully opened on October 2, 1865 by the Alton, Alresford and Winchester Railway with its southern terminus at Winchester and not Southampton. Its northern terminus was at Alton. The railway was 17 miles (27km) in length, standard gauge and single track with passing loops at intermediate stations and was operated by the London & South Western Railway (LSWR) who eventually bought the line in 1884.

Alton was an interchange station for onward travel using the Alton Line via Brookwood to London Waterloo and also provided connections to the Basingstoke and Alton Light Railway and the Meon Valley Line at Butts Junction just south of Alton. About two and a half miles (4km) before reaching Winchester station was Winchester Junction where the line joined the LSWR Basingstoke/Southampton main line for its run into Winchester and then immediately across a bridge over the standard gauge, single track of the Didcot, Newbury and Southampton Railway (DNSR).

This line, which was a GWR project, did

This photo, circa 1950, at Shawford Junction is looking in the Winchester direction with a mixed freight train behind a 4-6-0 Class S15 heading towards Southampton on the Southern Railway (ex LSWR) main line. Branching in from the right at the signal box is the GWR (Didcot, Newbury & Southampton Railway) line having left Winchester Chesil station.

not call at Winchester station but called at a separate station to the east of the city called Winchester (Chesil). At that time this line never reached Southampton and was truncated just south of the city where it joined the LSWR at Shawford Junction. At this point was a GWR signal box and GWR signals on the double track LSWR main line!

The Mid Hants Line as it was called ran through the agricultural chalk hills of Hampshire, locally named 'The Alps' because of some steep gradients along the line; the steepest gradient being 1:60 in the Medstead and Four Marks area.

The chalk hills, valleys and pure water streams have always been the domain of the

This photo was also taken on the GWR (DNSR) line at an unknown location circa 1950, and shows the single running track heading south towards Shawford Junction (left) and north, under the bridge, towards Winchester Chesil. The GWR signals have white diamond indicators telling a driver that the next section of line has a track circuit connected to the local signal box and under certain circumstances can proceed past the stop signal (shunting etc). The track circuit automatically indicates train movement to the signalman.

Unknown location of a LSWR 0-4-4, Class M7 No. 30052. These locomotives were the mainstay on the Mid Hants Railway and were modified to operate with push-pull capabilities. A total of 105 locomotives were built at Nine Elms Works to a Dugald Drummond design between 1897 and 1911. The last M7s were withdrawn from service in 1964.

Hampshire watercress growers and the new line gave them the opportunity to expand their businesses, taking their watercress to the local station by horse and cart, then transferring to faster rail services into London's Covent Garden market. The Mid Hants Railway became known as the 'Watercress Line'.

With the growing success and the population growth of London and its suburbs, the line from Waterloo station to Alton was electrified in 1937 as part of the Southern Region 650V third rail expansion programme. This relegated the line to a minor role although the watercress traffic was still loaded onto passenger trains from Alresford to Alton with easy onwards transfer to London.

Whenever there were any major engineering works on the Southern Railway main line, trains were diverted down the 'Watercress Line'. This branch line also played its part in the last war as heavy military traffic from the Aldershot district (Army Camps) ran to the Southampton Docks via Alton and Winchester and Southern Railway route.

From the early days passenger trains ran as push-pull, two carriage units, that did not require the locomotive to run round its train at the terminus. Instead, the fireman remained in the locomotive to maintain the fire and the driver ran the train back again from the end of the last carriage using a primitive cable and pulley system specially installed between the locomotive and the end carriage.

The locomotive normally used was the Drummond-designed LSWR class M7, 0-4-4 tank of which 105 were built at Nine Elms, London, in the period 1897 to 1911 and 31 M7s were equipped for push-pull operation. They used Westinghouse braking systems with the distinctive sound of their double pumps. They were originally designed for the LSWR London suburban traffic, at which they excelled, until they were gradually replaced by the spread of the SR third rail electrification programme following the Big Four grouping of 1923. This resulted in several of the M7s finding new stamping grounds in the Hampshire countryside and branch lines in the West Country.

Freight traffic on the line was sparse, serving the farming communities with a majority of freight traffic emanating from the watercress growers. Locomotives on freight duties included another of Drummond's designs, the successful Class 700, 0-6-0 goods engines built in 1897, with several surviving into the 1960s. This class of goods engine also worked on freight trains from the Midlands area via the Didcot, Newbury and Southampton Railway (DNSR) to Winchester Chesil station. Also working pick-up goods in later days were the BR Class 4 2-6-4 tanks. In

An example of a LSWR Class 700, 0-6-0 locomotive No. 30700, seen here at the BR (ex SR) shed at Eastleigh, Hampshire in March 1964. It is another Dugald Drummond design and used mainly for freight movements and could be seen on the Mid Hants line. A total of 30 locomotives were built between March and June 1897 and were withdrawn from service between 1957 and 1962 and none were saved for preservation.

During the 1950s, BR 2-6-4 standard Class 4 tank locomotives could be seen carrying out the reducing freight duties on the Mid Hants line. A total of 155 were built between 1951 and 1956 and were in operation across all regions except Western Region. This fine preserved example is No. 80078 is on the Swanage heritage line in Dorset and was taken out of BR service in 1965.

1957, diesel locomotives made their presences known and only a year later closure notices were posted for the Watercress Line. It finally closed to traffic in February 1973.

This action by British Railways galvanised many interested people into a group who were determined to preserve as much of the delightful branch line as they could. Unfortunately it was not possible for the preservationists to go all the way to Winchester as the major M3 motorway was in the way and the cost was prohibitive. Alresford is

now the terminus at the southern end of the line and is the busiest and most popular station with most passenger facilities including shops, museum and café, plus it is on the town's doorstep. Most of the carriage stock is stored on adjacent sidings.

Ropley has the line's engineering centre and locomotive maintenance and running sheds. The platform area has flowerbeds and a couple of ornamental trees that have been carefully cut and maintained over the years, although originally there were three. The first train to run on

Alton station clearly showing the Network Rail platforms for South West Trains to London Waterloo on the left with a Class 450 Desiro EMU waiting to leave. Separated by the green fence is the Mid Hants line with 4-4-0 SR Schools class *Cheltenham* No. 30925 just arrived from the Alresford direction.

A busy scene at Medstead and Four Marks station in September 2007 with a mixed goods train and a passenger train headed up by a Southern Region 4-4-0 V Schools Class No. 30926 *Repton*.

the revived line was hauled by SR Class U No. 31806 from Alresford to Ropley then two years later to Alton.

Medstead and Four Marks station is the usual passing place for the trains. The line's technical departments are located here; Signal & Telegraph, Permanent Way and Buildings. It

is also the highest station in Hampshire!

Alton station is shared with the National Rail Network that provides service to London Waterloo where they have two platforms and Mid Hants Railway have one with two passing loops outside the station that can be used during peak times. Butts triple junction

A morning chat as the crew changes at Medsted & Four Marks with a BR standard 2MT 2-6-2T No. 41312 waiting to take out its next train in April 2007. It was built at Crewe Works during May 1952 and was withdrawn from service in July 1967. Its last shed was Templecombe in Somerset. It was rescued from Barry scrapyard in 1974 for preservation.

An example of a SR Merchant Navy Class locomotive, *Canadian Pacific*, pulling into Medsted & Four Marks station in 2007. It is a Pacific Class 4-6-2 built to a Bulleid design at Eastleigh Works in 1941 with air smoothed casing, but was rebuilt without it in 1959 and has clocked up just under a million miles.

A Maunsell designed, Southern Railway, Q Class 0-6-0 No. 30541 seen here heading up a mixed goods train by Chawton Park Woods in February 2016. This locomotive was built in 1939, withdrawn in 1964 and taken to Barry scrapyard where it was recovered for preservation being the only example of the class to survive.

Retiring to the shed at Ropley in 2007 are two GWR locomotives fronted by GWR Class 3200 (Earl Class), 4-4-0 *Earl of Berkeley* No. 9017, built in 1938 from a combination of Duke Class boiler on Bulldog frames and nicknamed Dukedog. It retired from BR service in 1965 and is just one of two remaining locomotives of this type, the other being *City of Truro*. Behind is GWR Class 4200 2-8-0T, number not known, but 100 were built at Swindon Works between 1923 and 1940.

is no more as the Meon Valley Line closed in 1955 and the Basingstoke and Alton Line closed in 1932.

The preservationists have done an excellent job in maintaining the Southern Railway atmosphere with locomotives such as Bulleid's West Country and Battle of Britain pacific classes, plus SR N and U class 2-6-0s,

both retrieved from the Barry scrapyard. When the Mid Hants line was reopened, *Errol Lonsdale*, 0-6-0 Austerity tank and another from the Longmoor Military Railway also in Hampshire were acquired, but this most interesting private line is also now closed. The latter loco, a 350hp diesel, now resides in Belgium.

A very atmospheric view of Alresford station in gloomy weather during 2020 with the BR standard 2MT 2-6-2T No. 41312 just about to leave with a mixed freight train. The SR signal is clear in its lower quadrant position to enable the train to proceed.

The now preserved Mid Hants branch line from Winchester to Alton, better known as The Watercress line; the station shown here is Ropley as it was with majestic topiary.

The 0-4-0 saddle tank standard gauge loco built by Thomas Spittle of Newport, Wales, for the Devon Great Consols Mine to Moorwellham Quay on the River Tamar, Devon.

Morwellham Quay

This very atmospheric scene is looking upstream on the River Tamar with Morwellham Quay on the right hand bank and in the distance is the overshot waterwheel. It was not an easily accessible location with steep hills rising from behind the village, so it was understandable that incline planes were a necessity in those times.

On the county border between Devon and Cornwall is the tidal river Tamar which meanders between wooded hills and gorges and was in the heartland of historic mineral extraction. Morwellham is about 23 miles (37km) upstream from the sea at Plymouth and just three miles (4.8km) downstream from the town of Tavistock that back in the 1300s was in Europe's richest tin mining area.

The lands bordering the river Tamar were in the ownership of the Duke of Bedford who leased some 167 acres to a consortium in 1844. A mine was opened, titled the Devon Great Consols Mine, which sank numerous shafts to

The Devon Great Consols Mine had two similar 0-4-0ST locomotives, *Hugo* and *Ada* built by Thomas Spittle Ltd of Newport in 1882 and were painted green with yellow coach lining. This poor photo is believed to show *Hugo*.

This view across the river to Morwellham Quay plainly shows the layout of the quays and the elevated trestle standard gauge rail track for the Devon Great Consols Mine. The tracks fan out from one raised point at the rear of the quayside where one track exits the tunnel that goes back under the cottages and then rises up the hill via the incline, directly behind. The line of the incline can be seen although densely wooded. The canal for barges feeding the second incline plane can be seen by the straight and level row of trees going to the right from the house half way up the hill.

extract copper ore and would eventually become the world's largest producer of copper. Arsenic is also found in this general area stretching onto Dartmoor.

Joseph Hitchens, who took the lease, became the instigator for further development of the mine and its resources. With increased production of the ore, it became necessary to have it transported by railway. A five mile (8km) standard gauge line was built with sidings at the several mine shafts and a half mile (0.8km) incline from the top of the hills down to Morwellham where the line passed under Bedford Cottages using a short tunnel that emerged at the quayside where the Devon Great Consols Mine had its own dock and sidings that were on raised wooden trestles.

The wagons were drawn up and down the incline using a wire rope powered by a

stationary steam engine located at the head of the incline. Bedded into the surface around the quayside areas are the remains of the standard gauge track to the base of the incline where several different types of rail were laid into stone blocks as was the custom in those times. At the top of the incline, which runs up through dense woods, the line turned on the level to head north where it passed under a local road from Tavistock to Gulworthy.

The Devon Great Consols Mine had several shafts which were driven to a depth of 110m, with a total of 12, some of which were for arsenic and a little tin extraction. Pumping stations were required to remove water and so coal was brought back to the mine to fire the steam boilers. At the mine itself there was around one mile of sidings. There were 350 employees at the time of closure on May 31, 1901, but when in full operation the mine had had some 1,300 employees, which puts

A third locomotive at the Devon Great Consols Mine was an 0-4-0T of unknown manufacturer, but unfortunately records of their locomotives are incomplete.

into perspective the enormity of the mining operation.

There were two 0-4-0 saddle tank locomotives built by Thomas Spittle Ltd of Newport, Wales, named *Hugo* and *Ada*. They were painted green with yellow coach lining in a very professional manner, clearly indicating the importance of these grand locos in such a remote and sparsely populated area of Devon. The locos had 2ft 3in wheels driven by 10in cylinders.

As well as rail connection to the mines a 4.5 mile (7.2km) canal, fed from the River Tavy, was constructed from Tavistock and opened in 1805. It was 16ft (4.9m) wide and 3ft (0.9m) deep and ran through a 2,540yd (2.32km) tunnel under Morwell Down and over an aqueduct that carried it above the River Lumburn. It was built with a very small incline allowing a constant flow of water to assist the small barges on their way to Morwellham. They carried silver-lead ore, iron, timber, slate

Today, this piece of track has been laid on the original stone blocks to identify the route taken for the standard gauge line to and from the quayside.

A reconstruction of the elevated trestle railway track can be seen on either side of the dock area with a couple of the wagons of the type in use at the time.

Again, a reconstruction of one of the quays with a boat to create the atmosphere of those times and a wooden derrick is on the left.

and copper from mines whose machinery was powered by water wheels alongside the canal.

The canal ended 237ft (72m) above the quay at Morwellham, which necessitated a steep incline plane with two tracks. One track transferred goods to the quay for loading onto the awaiting boats and the other track ended some 30ft

(9.1m) higher at ore chutes above the Lower Copper Quay. This operation was accomplished by small four-wheeled tipping wagons that operated independently on the two inclines and powered by an overshot waterwheel using water from the canal. The rails were cast iron, L-shaped and gauged at 46in (1.1684m).

The small port of Morwellham grew, with

This shows the Tavistock canal on a pleasant autumn day with the hills dropping away to the left. There wasn't too much room for barges passing each other. The barges were shallow draught and the canal depth was a maximum of 3ft (0.9m) with a maximum width of 16ft (4.9m). The canal followed the contours of the hillsides to prevent using locks to raise and lower the canal levels.

cottages provided for the many workers, with a small chapel, shop and of course the Ship Inn, which still functions to this day. On the level beside the docks were several lime kilns and a small copper mine which headed straight into the heavily wooded hill above; this is open to the public and has a narrow gauge railway to take visitors inside to see how the mine once worked. On the quayside are some replica wagons of the type once used by the mines.

Fairly large sailing ships of around 200 tons sailed up from Plymouth Sound to Morwellham which was the limit of navigation for ships of that size, but by 1903 the Great Western Railway and London and South Western Railway had their own railway stations in Tavistock and business gradually drifted away from the Morwellham Quay.

Nothing is operational today but the reconstructed quayside, boat, four-wheeled wagons and 32ft (9.75m) overshot water wheel once used for crushing manganese, adds to the atmosphere.

This is a train ride into the George and Charlotte copper mine that operated in the 18th and 19th centuries. The trip is educational and takes around 40 minutes. On exiting from the underground mine the trip continues along the picturesque Tamar valley before returning. The small locomotive is battery driven.

The Railways of North Norfolk

Seaside towns along the Norfolk coast were once well served with railways from Lowestoft to Sheringham, the Norfolk Broads and King's Lynn, but nearly all have closed apart from the Bittern Line from Norwich to Cromer and Sheringham and the main line from London Liverpool Street to King's Lynn, both on the national network. However, not all is lost!

Bittern Line

The Bittern Line as it is now called is part of the National Rail, standard gauge network. It is a rural branch line running for 30 miles (48km) from Norwich to Sheringham on the North Norfolk coast and was opened between 1874 and 1877. It was named Bittern after the rare bird that is found in and around the flat wetlands of the Norfolk Broads. Until recently, Greater Anglia operated Class 153 & 156 diesel Sprinters plus Class 170 Turbostars. These have now been replaced by Class 755s

manufactured by Stadler of Switzerland and are one of their FLIRT series, Fast Light Intercity Regional Trains.

There are 10 stations along the line from Norwich, which is the connection for the Great Eastern Main Line, the Breckland line and Wherry lines. The double track line heads north, crossing the rivers Yare and Bure with the first major stop being Hoveton & Wroxham, the station for the popular Norfolk Broads. It is also the connection for the Bure Valley 15in (381mm) gauge heritage railway. From Hoveton & Wroxham station the line is single track.

Further on is Gunton station, 19.9 miles (31.8km) from Norwich. The station is in the middle of the countryside with no villages in the immediate area. However, there was a reason for its location, as it was built mainly for the convenience of Lord Suffield who was a major investor in the original East Norfolk Railway, which built the line from Norwich to Cromer. He owned and lived in

Gunton station, opened on July 29, 1876, is in an isolated spot on the Bittern Line with just a couple of parking spaces. The original station building has been beautifully restored back to its original condition and is now privately owned. The original loop line to serve that platform has been removed and a safety fence installed. The running platform by comparison is just a basic concrete structure, a couple of seats and a very basic shelter.

Having reversed out of the platform at Cromer, the Class 156 No. 156419 arrives at its destination in Sheringham, being the end of the line, and comes to a stop just 50yds (45.7m) from the level crossing that separates Network Rail from the preserved North Norfolk Railway.

Gunton Hall about one and a half miles (2.4km) from the station. Royal guests regularly used the station including Lily Langtry, the mistress of the Prince of Wales (later King Edward VII) who liaised with her at the Estate's second house, Stewards Farm. This is now the highly recommended pub/hotel, Gunton Arms.

The original station house, although not in use, has been privately bought and restored to its original splendid condition. It cannot be accessed by rail as the loop track has been lifted and a plain straightforward platform with a small shelter is provided on the adjacent running line.

The next important stop is Cromer Beach, a dead end

A view looking from the end of the NR Sheringham platform towards the level crossing separating Network Rail from the North Norfolk Railway. The Sheringham East signal box can be seen on the far side with the original Midland & Great Northern Joint Railway (M&GNJR) station on the far right, which is now the Sheringham station for the North Norfolk Railway.

One of the new bi-mode Stadler Class 755-4s now operating on most local routes in the Greater Anglia area. They are three- or four-car units with a smaller power car located in the middle of the train that house the Deutz V8 diesel engines and generators. The pantographs for 25kV AC 50 cycles overhead line operation are mounted on intermediate cars. Each car shares a bogie unit (Jacobs bogie) with the adjoin car to provide a smooth ride.

A 1959 photo of Melton Constable station looking eastwards towards Sheringham, Cromer and Great Yarmouth and Norwich to the right. The locomotive taking on water is a Class B12/3 4-6-0, originally built as Great Eastern Railway (GER) Class S69 and later reclassified as B12 by LNER. Seventy-one locomotives were built with a majority being built at the Stratford Works.

and 26¾ miles (42.8km) from Norwich. Cromer has always been a popular holiday destination since Victorian times and once boasted another station – Cromer High Road – which has since been closed. Unlike attractive Gunton station, Cromer is run down and neglected. The station building is closed completely and the station comprises an island platform, with entry for passengers from

one end, and a track either side. Trains from Norwich enter on one platform and reverse out to continue to Sheringham. The train is then switched to the Sheringham line outside the station area.

Sheringham is the end of the line as far as the National Network is concerned. It is a single platform with a small shelter and a ticket machine. The line ends a few feet (metres) away

from the level crossing gates at the top of Sheringham's main street. The other side of the gates is the North Norfolk Heritage Railway.

The North Norfolk Railway (NNR)

Going back to 1887, Cromer could also be reached from

west Norfolk from a 15¾ mile (25.2km) line from Melton Constable, a busy railway hub, via Sheringham as part of the Midland and Great Northern Joint Railway (M&GNJR). Melton Constable was locally named 'The Crewe of Norfolk' because of it being a junction of several local lines and extensive railway workshops. Its network

Looking down the tracks from the level crossing towards Holt adequately indicates how well the original M&GNJR Sheringham station has been restored showing the luggage, which were mainly trunks, that could be sent on ahead of the passengers to be at the hotels or guest houses ready for the arrival of the owners. The rest of the station furniture and the signals in the background add to the atmosphere of times gone by.

This fine example of an ex-WD Austerity 2-8-0 No. 90775 was built by the North British Railway Company in 1943 and saw service in the Middle East and then 27 years working for Hellenic Railways. It was repatriated back to Ipswich in 1984 and has worked on the North Norfolk Railway since 2003 and named as *The Royal Norfolk Regiment* in 2017.

The 2-8-0 No. 90755 seen here pulling away with a full train from Sheringham October 2019 on its way along the Norfolk coast to the current terminus at Holt just 5¼miles (8.4km) from Sheringham.

reached across north Norfolk and west to south Lincolnshire to Spalding and Peterborough.

Fortunately, neither Cromer nor Sheringham were singled out for closure in the Beeching Report of 1964, but British Rail (BR) wanted to eliminate the level crossing at Sheringham as

BR had closed the line to Melton Constable. To achieve this, BR closed the original Sheringham station, lifted the track across the level crossing and built a new unattractive utilitarian single platform on the Cromer side of the crossing.

In 1965 a volunteer group

Looking down the platform at Holt station. This is not the original station as that was in Holt village and was shut down by Dr Beeching in 1964. The new Holt station is outside Holt and station building is the original from Stalham that was rebuilt, brick by brick. The station area has a small goods yard and goods shed, which is now a museum for the M&GNJR.

formed North Norfolk Railway plc and was granted two Light Railway Orders and so work commenced to rebuild the single track line and its infrastructure. The line is just over five miles (8km) in length and terminates at the attractive Georgian town of Holt with two intermediate stations at Weybourne and Kelling Heath. During June 1967 two locomotives were delivered and the railway has continued to increase its rolling stock.

Until 2010 there was no connection between the national network and the NNR, although they were only separated by a few yards (metres). After agreement between all parties, this situation was soon to be reversed and volunteers reinstated the level crossing with new track connecting both railways. On March 11, 2010, BR Britannia Class 4-6-2 Pacific No. 70013 *Oliver Cromwell* slowly pulled a special train from Kings Cross via Norwich over the new crossing into NNRs Sheringham station. It continued to its final destination at Holt. The crossing is not in regular use but is a wonderful advantage for special trains and visiting locomotives to visit the NNR.

Aylsham South station was on the East Norfolk Railway from Wroxham. The station was opened in 1880 and closed in 1981 and demolished in 1989 to make way for the Aylsham terminus of the narrow gauge Bure Valley Line. This photo dated around the early 1950s shows a GER Holden designed Class E4 2-4-0, No. 62797 built in 1902 at Stratford Works about to leave with its train for Wroxham. The locomotive was withdrawn from service in 1958.

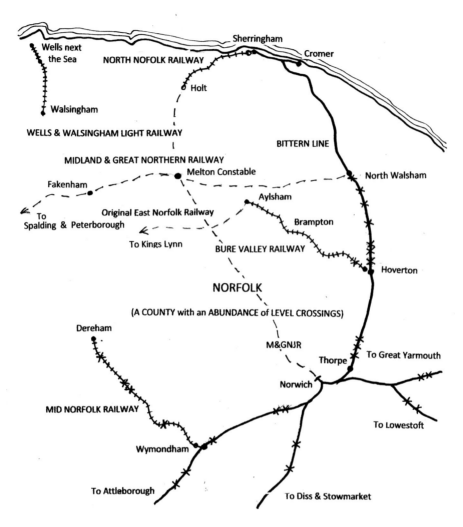

Wells next the Sea

Sherringham

Cromer

NORTH NOFOLK RAILWAY

Holt

WELLS & WALSINGHAM LIGHT RAILWAY

Walsingham

BITTERN LINE

MIDLAND & GREAT NORTHERN RAILWAY

Melton Constable

North Walsham

Fakenham

Aylsham

To Spalding & Peterborough

Original East Norfolk Railway

Brampton

To Kings Lynn

BURE VALLEY RAILWAY

NORFOLK

Hoverton

(A COUNTY with an ABUNDANCE of LEVEL CROSSINGS)

Dereham

M&GNJR

Thorpe

To Great Yarmouth

Norwich

MID NORFOLK RAILWAY

To Lowestoft

Wymondham

To Attleborough

To Diss & Stowmarket

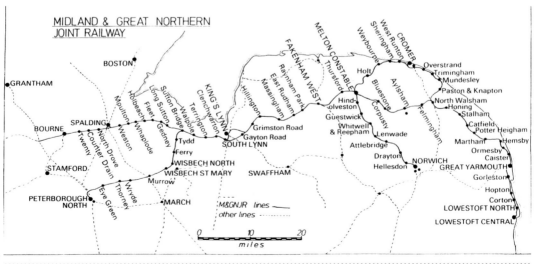

MIDLAND & GREAT NORTHERN JOINT RAILWAY

BOSTON

GRANTHAM

MELTON CONSTABLE

FAKENHAM WEST

Sheringham

West Runton

CROMER

Weybourne

Overstrand
Trimingham
Mundesley
Paston & Knapton

Holt

Bluestone

Aylsham

North Walsham
Honing
Stalham

Raynham park
East Rudham
Massingham

Thursford

Hind-olveston

Corpusty

Felmingham

KING'S LYNN
Clenchwarton

Hillington

Guestwick

Catfield
Potter Heigham

Whitwell
& Reepham

Lenwade

SPALDING

Sutton Bridge

Walsole

Grimston Road

Marthan
Hemsby

BOURNE

Moulton

Weston

Terrington

Gayton Road
SOUTH LYNN

Attlebridge

Ormesby
Caister

Holbeach
Long Sutton
Fleet
Gedney

Tydd
Ferry

Drayton
Hellesdon

NORWICH

GREAT YARMOUTH

North Drove
Counter Drain
Twenty

WISBECH NORTH
WISBECH ST MARY

SWAFFHAM

Gorleston

STAMFORD

Murrow

Hopton
Corton
LOWESTOFT NORTH

PETERBOROUGH NORTH

Wryde
Thorney
Eye Green

MARCH

M&GNJR lines ———
other lines - - - - - -

LOWESTOFT CENTRAL

0   10   20
miles

Greater Anglia Railways took delivery of 111 units of the Aventra 720 Class EMUs in 2020, built by Bombardier UK, one seen here in the Essex countryside which they serve.

Bure Valley Railway

As the Bure Valley Railway terminus is only a very short walk across a footbridge from Hoveton & Wroxham station it deserves some explanation. In fact this 15in (381mm) narrow gauge railway is built on the old track bed of the standard gauge East Norfolk Railway (ENR) that commenced services in 1877 from Norwich to Cromer with a nine mile (14.4km) branch from Wroxham to Aylsham in 1880. In common with a lot of small branch lines

Bure Valley 15in (381mm) gauge locomotive No. 1 *Wroxham Broad* about to leave Wroxham station. This is a 2-6-4T locomotive painted in Caledonian blue and was originally built in 1964 as a 2-6-2T powered by an internal combustion engine. It was rebuilt as a steam locomotive in 1992.

This locomotive, built in 1994 is No. 6 *Blickling Hall*, a 2-6-2 ZB Class tender locomotive inspired by Indian Railways, painted in Great Eastern Railway blue. It is seen here just easing itself off the turntable at Wroxham station and blowing off steam. In the background is the original 50 lever Wroxham signal box built by Mckenzie and Holland in 1900 to GER design, and closed in 2000. Behind the signal box can be seen the canopy of Wroxham Network Rail station.

it did not pay its way and passenger traffic ceased in 1952. Most freight traffic had followed by 1974, with the track being lifted by 1984.

The track bed from Wroxham to Aylsham was initially purchased by Broadland District Council for a footpath but a number of railway enthusiasts on the council suggested that a narrow gauge railway and a footpath could both be accommodated across the width of the old track bed. The council then went into partnership with some theme park owners of Great Yarmouth and construction began in 1989 and was ready for the grand opening in 1990. Locomotives were hired from the Romney

Hythe and Dymchurch Railway.

Unfortunately, the following 10 years with five different owners did not bode well for the stability of the railway until 2001 when the line was bought by a group of railway enthusiasts with business backgrounds. Since then the railway has gone from strength to strength and has five steam locomotives, three diesel locomotives and an assortment of well-appointed coaches. Both Wroxham and Aylsham have turntables, so that all locomotives can be front facing. There are three intermediate halts after leaving Wroxham; Brampton, Buxton and Coltishall.

This is the first locomotive purchased by the brewery and called *Mendip*. It was built by Bagnall in 1903 and was an 0-4- 0ST, Works No. 1701 and sported green livery.

In the delightful rolling farmland of Somerset is the village of Oakhill, renowned for many years as the home of the celebrated Oakhill Stout beer. The brewery was founded in 1767 and managed a buoyant and growing trade of its popular beers, with its stout being sold as far afield as London.

The brewery was despatching around 2,200 barrels, of 36 gallons

The second locomotive to be purchased by the brewery was *Oakhill* and delivered in 1904. It was an 0-4-0ST, Works No. 1021 and built by Peckett and Son. It is seen here at the brewery with a train consisting of three bogie wagons, the far two with barrels of beer and the one nearest the locomotive with crates of beer covered with a tarpaulin.

(164 litres) per week, so in 1899 it acquired a single cylinder Wallis & Stevens steam road vehicle with two solid-wheeled trailers, principally to transport the beer to the goods yard at the Somerset & Dorset Joint Railway station at Binegar. The station was 17¼ miles (26.6km) south of Bath. The heavy loads hauled by the steam tractor caused damage to the lightly built local roads and complaints from the local Authority prompted the brewery to invest in its own private railway to connect the Oakhill Brewery and Maltings to Binegar station.

Oakhill Brewery purchased two locomotives; the first in 1903 was W. G. Bagnall 0-4-0ST, Works No. 1701 and named *Mendip*. The second was in 1904, a Peckett 0-4-0T Works No. 1021 and named *Oakhill*.

The private 2¾ mile (4.4km) railway was laid to 2ft 6in (760mm) gauge and was completed in 1903. It never carried passengers, except a few unofficial school children and a few employees, so it did not require Parliamentary sanction. The track was laid with 56lb per yard, flat-bottom rails spiked directly to transverse wooden sleepers. On leaving the brewery, from the centre of the village, the railway climbed on a gradient of 1 in 30 across grazing fields.

About a mile onward the single track crossed the Shepton Mallet to Bristol A37 road on the level, with a short refuge siding available should the locomotive slip in wet conditions pulling a full load. This allowed a few wagons to be uncoupled and collected later. Near the Mendip Inn (owned by the brewery) the track crossed over the Wells road. A short distance onward at Binegar Bottom it faced its only major engineering feature

– a three span steel girder viaduct that carried the railway 35ft (10.7m) above a minor road. Terminating at Binegar station the narrow gauge entered a stone built exchange shed on the down side of the main line. This shed was equipped with a two ton timber crane to assist in the transfer of the heavy wooden casks onto an adjacent standard gauge siding where eight ton wooden wagons awaited their load of beer.

Running time uphill to Binegar was approximately 256 minutes, with suitable long blasts on the loco's whistle when approaching the road level crossings. The return journey 'down hill' was just 20 minutes where coal was frequently transported back to the brewery and

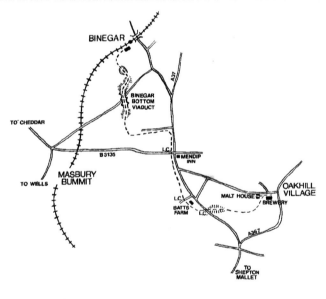

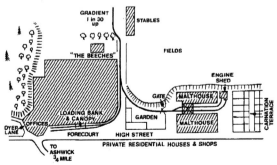

DIAGRAM OF THE RAILWAY SERVING THE OAKHILL BREWERY; c 1920.

This is *Oakhill* slowly crossing the viaduct that spans Binegar Bottom with a short train of just two bogie wagons of the 'precious' cargo en route to Binegar station.

malthouses to fire their boilers and to maintain a coal stock for the locomotives.

During the First World War, trade began to decline due to the limitations of raw materials and labour shortages. After 1918 and peace, trade improved, but by that time road transport was rapidly developing and the widespread use of motor lorries pushed the owners into investing in brewery drays. The outcome of this was that the railway was discontinued in 1921. The track was laid largely on land owned by the brewery, so this was lifted and the viaduct and one bridge were

dismantled. The two steam locos were sold, with *Oakhill* working anew at the Portland Cement Co at Penarth.

In 1924 the brewery was severely damaged by fire, but fortunately the large malthouses were separated from the brewery buildings and remained intact, with the business being taken over by the Bristol United Breweries, later to become a part of the Courage Group. Malting continued here well into the 1980s. In 1984 the phoenix arose once again as a small micro-brewery commenced brewing using the old title. Their beers also reflected the 'good old

A view of Binegar station (Ex S&DJR) looking in the Bath direction in much later days showing the old Oakhill Brewery trans-shipment shed to the right, no longer in use and the rails long gone.

Inside the old Oakhill Brewery trans-shipment shed with the timber crane still in reasonable condition. The brewery's narrow gauge railway terminated inside the shed. The standard gauge goods yard would have been to the right and most of that has disappeared.

A photo of the brewery with its train and staff stood to attention for the posed photograph. This shows four bogie wagons fully loaded with casks of beer and headed up by *Oakhill* ready to leave for its trip to Binegar station.

days' of the Oakhill Brewery as their beers were named Mendip Gold, Mendip Twister, Yeoman, and the once famous Original

Stout. Sadly this rather remote micro-brewery closed in 2004.

After the little railway was closed the Oakhill Brewery bought some steam motor wagons. This one was a Garrett 6 Tonner No. 34386 built in 1923, registration number BJ 8598. This one had a trailer and there was solid tyres all round.

Oakhill Brewery narrow gauge train of full beer casks bound for Binegar, about to cross over the viaduct at Binegar Bottom before arriving at the S&DJR interchange.

This photo taken in 1959 shows a four coach train approaching Masbury Summit headed up by a 4-4-0 Class 2P-B No. 40700, built at Crewe Works on December 31, 1932 and was withdrawn on September 30, 1962 after 30 years' service. It was based at Bath Shed 71G.

Somerset is one of the largest counties in England, but is only half the size of Yorkshire. It is mainly rural with well-known places such as the Cheddar Gorge, Mendip Hills, Somerset Levels, and the City of Bath with its Roman Baths and sea-side towns like Weston-super-Mare. It has also had quite extensive coalfields and iron ore mines with many being once serviced by local railways. Today the main line just passes through it, apart from a heritage line! The following is a look back at the past and a few of the important railways of that time.

A fine example of a S&DJR 2-8-0 in preservation seen here at Medstead & Four Marks 1. This 1959 photo shows a four coach train approaching Masbury Summit. The locomotive is station on the Mid Hants Railway (Watercress Line) in September 2010. The S&DJR locomotive No. 88 was built by Robert Stephenson & Co. in 1925 and was one of five built that year. It was withdrawn from service during 1963.

A regular on the S&DJR was the LMS Fowler Class 3F 0-6-0T locomotive used mainly for freight work and was one of seven built by W.G. Bagnall in 1929 with S&D numbers 19-25, later numbered 7310-7316. This example, in preservation is not an ex S&DJR locomotive.

Somerset and Dorset Joint Railway

As the name suggests the Somerset & Dorset Joint Railway (S&DJR) was an amalgamation of the Somerset Central Railway (SCR) and the Dorset Central Railway (DCR). Like all railways in the 1800s they had their own agendas on expansion of lines, profits and destinations and so on, but the past has proved that a majority of these 'small' railways needed to amalgamate for their longer term expectations to be realised.

The SCR started life in 1854 by providing a local broad gauge 7¼ft (2,140mm) link between Highbridge Wharf on the Bristol Channel, 18 miles (28.8km) to Glastonbury for the merchants

The North Dorset Railway Trust has made a great job of reconstructing Shillingstone station, recreating the atmosphere of those S&DJR days with the station master's garden, tea room, signal box and level crossing.

A train, hauled by a BR standard Class 3, bound for Bath halts at Shillingstone station sometime before 1966. This photograph clearly shows the original signal box and Porters Lodge.

Shillingstone station in preservation era with Porters Lodge and the replica signal box that has been equipped with the correct Stevens, 14 lever frame and Tyer's electronic train tablet machines. A single home signal is located at the end of the up platform, as originally there were sidings and a loop into the down platform.

of that town, as it was a vibrant manufacturing centre and they needed to transport their goods to the Bristol Channel ports and have access to the wide gauge Bristol and Exeter Railway main line.

Beyond Glastonbury a short branch north was opened to the City of Wells in 1859 with a view to extending east from there to Frome for a connection with the Wilts, Somerset and Weymouth

Railway with access to the south coast towns. However, that never materialised and a more direct route was sought by a link to Cole and a running arrangement with the Dorset Central Railway.

The Dorset Central Railway (DCR) opened for business in 1860 from the London and South Western Railway (LSWR) station at Wimborne to Blandford; it was standard gauge and worked by the LSWR. Similar to the SCR,

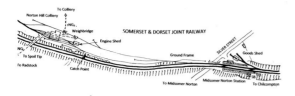

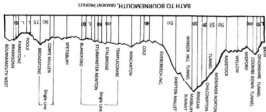

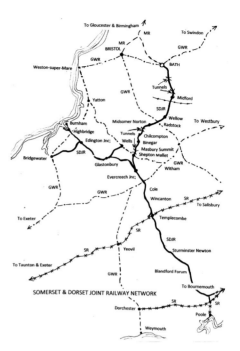

The Somerset & Dorset Joint Railway in all its splendour of deep blue livery for both coaches and locomotives, seen with a local train in lovely countryside.

they had aspirations to expand, but in a northerly direction. So, joining with the SCR was a way for both companies to realise their expectations.

The SCR and DCR were amalgamated in 1862 to become the Somerset and Dorset Railway (S&DR) and the line ran from Burnham-on-Sea, North Somerset, on the Bristol Channel coast, south to Wimborne in Dorset by which time all track had been converted to Standard gauge. From Wimborne station S&DR ran on London and South Western Railway (LSWR) metals to Hamworthy, which is a part of Poole in Dorset and along the south coast close to Bournemouth. They anticipated high monetary returns for this cross country route between the South Coast and the Bristol Channel, but that didn't happen and they soon found themselves in financial difficulties.

Looking north at Shillingstone with both tracks occupied with the two diesel shunters. On the left is resident Ruston Hornsby 48DS Class 4wDDM, No. DS1169, built in 1951, named *Little Eva*. On the right is a Hudswell Clarke 0-6-0DM, No. D1186, built in 1959 and named *Ashdown* that was delivered in 2020.

The following photographs were taken at Midsomer Norton station, home of the S&DR Heritage Trust on a rather grey day in 2020. It is the terminus and only station on the short one mile (1.6km) line and shows a view down the platform.

A Class 03, 0-6-0DH, No. D2128, was built at BR Works, Swindon on January 7, 1961 and had a chequered life, being sold for scrap in 1976, then sold onto a Belgium company who rebuilt the locomotive and it ended up in a railway museum in 1989. In 1993 it went to Peak Rail and then on to the Corus Steel Works at Scunthorpe during 2008. It now resides at Midsomer Norton.

The S&DJR had two Sentinel steam locomotives (7587 & 7588) built in 1929. They had vertical boilers, were chain driven and used for shunting coal wagons at collieries around Radstock. Unfortunately, neither of these locomotives survives, but they have a similar one from Croydon Gasworks, 0-4-0 4W with vertical boiler and two transverse engines No. 7109 named *Joyce* which has now been restored to full operational use.

To try and avoid receivership a decision was made to build a new line from Evercreech Junction to Bath joining up with the Midland Railway (MR), so opening up a through route from the South Coast to the Midlands and North of England. It was successful, but too late to avoid going into receivership and in 1875 the line was taken over jointly by the MR and LSWR and became the Somerset and Dorset Joint Railway (S&DJR). Going north the new line passed through Midsomer Norton and Radstock, which was becoming an important industrial area with many collieries at the start of the 1900s. There were eight collieries and other industries including five milk processing factories and six stone quarries all with private sidings provided to move the raw materials to Bath, Bristol and beyond. Many other industrial businesses had similar arrangements along the line.

Following the 1923 grouping it came under the joint management of the London Midland and Scottish Railway (LMS) and the Southern Railway (SR).

The line became a part of British Rail from 1948 and regular services ran between Manchester and Bournemouth, being especially busy during summer months with long distance trains such as the 'Pines Express', so called after the pine trees around Bournemouth. This train had been running regularly since 1927. There were tunnels, valleys and steep gradients that often required a banking locomotive for heavy passenger and freight trains, especially the 811ft (247m) climb up to Masbury. A great deal of the line in this area was single track with passing loops. This difficult part of the line through the Mendips earned the S&D line the nickname of 'Slow and Dirty'.

During the 50s and 60s, traffic on the line was gradually declining and the last 'Pines Express' was rerouted at the end of the summer season in 1962. Dr Beeching's Axe finally fell on March 7, 1966, closing the whole S&D line between Bournemouth and Bath.

A variety of locomotives found their way to the S&D, but the mainstay for many years was the Midland 4-4-0 Class 2P used mainly for passenger services and several variations of Midland Class 3F 0-6-0 tender locomotives and 0-6-0T locomotives for handling the freight. Also, Class 7F 2-8-0s built by Robert Stephenson & Co. of which 11 were built for the S&DJR from 1925 onwards. During the last few years until closure various GWR, LMS and BR locomotives were used including Class 9F 2-10-0 No. 92220 *Evening Star*, the last steam engine built by BR in 1960. S&DJR trains were virtually all steam hauled until its closure.

Little now remains, but efforts are being made to reconstruct short pieces of line and refurbish stations in a couple of places such as Shillingstone and Midsomer Norton.

Shillingstone station is just a few miles north-west of Blandford and great strides have be made by the North Dorset Railway Trust to totally reconstruct the station, signal box, cattle dock etc. and laid a short length of track together with some rolling stock to recreate the look and atmosphere of those past years. In fact, the loop line for the down platform has now been relaid and a planning application has been submitted to extend the line north to Cattle Creep Bridge.

The Somerset and Dorset Railway Heritage Trust has accomplished similar results at the station and yard at Midsomer Norton, which was further north on the SDJR and located part-way up the 1:50 gradient towards the Masbury summit. It has about a mile (1.6km) of track and several interesting items of rolling stock.

A nicely turned out 0-6-0 Class 08 diesel, No. D4095 built in 1961, sits silent in the station. It spent most of its working life in Scotland until 2004 then to the Gloucester & Warwick railway and then on to the quarry at Mount Sorrel. It came to the S&DR Trust in 2008.

The 'Pines Express' was renowned by many tourists from the north travelling to the southern resorts, here hauled by two West Country pacifics on the Somerset and Dorset Joint Railway in typical Somerset rolling countryside.

West Somerset Mineral Railway

As early as 1860 the harbour town of Watchet, situated on the south bank of the Bristol Channel, was enjoying increasing prosperity from the large quantities of iron ore being carried by vessels leaving the western quay. Transport to the quay would be necessitated by horse and cart having made their arduous journeys down from the outlying quarries in the Brendon Hills.

Fortunately, the transport of iron ore improved when, in 1861, a standard gauge, single track railway of 11½ miles (18.4km) in length was opened between Watchet harbour and the mines at the top of the Brendon Hills. The iron ore was shipped across the Bristol Channel to Newport, South Wales and then by rail to the Ebbw Vale Company steel mills. The West Somerset Mineral Railway was formed in 1855 by the proprietors of the Ebbw Vale

steel mills who had a monetary interest in the Brendon Hills iron Co. The railway opened for business in 1861 and as well as transporting the iron ore the railway also provided a passenger service that commenced in 1865.

The line left Watchet harbour and proceeded up the Wansford Valley, crossing the small river by a girder bridge to the first of the intermediate stations. After this the single track line skirted past the existing ruins of Cleeve Abbey and then via a cutting into the rock face to one side at the hamlet of Fair Cross at Torre Road level crossing. Here there was a single siding opposite the existing gatekeeper's hut dated 1871; each elevation of the brick hut has a small window lookout to all directions.

Next came another road crossing with gatekeeper's hut at Clitsome. From here the lush valley pastures are left behind as the gradient increases to 1:94 with the track following the river further inland. After Roadwater station the track wound its way

A passenger train consisting of two four-wheel coaches, at Coombe Row, seen standing at the bottom of the Brendon incline. Although a station of sorts was built at the top, the company decided not to spend money bringing the incline, station and track up to a standard to allow passengers to use the incline. Not to be outdone, the passengers hitched a ride on the wagons at their own risk. The locomotive is one of the Sharp Stewart 0-6-0ST. Photo circa 1880.

A view clearly showing the double track of the whole incline with an empty wagon at the bottom and it certainly looks a long 0.6 mile (1km) to the summit. Next to the wagon can be seen the early type disc and crossbar signal.

through a valley with an increasing gradient of 1:44 and then arrived at Comberow station at the bottom of a steep incline to the top of the Brendon Hills. The journey time from Watchet was 30 minutes. The incline of two tracks rose to a height of 800ft (244m) and with a length of 1,100yds (1,006m) long, giving a gradient of 1:4.

When built the lower levels of the valley were fields with the upper half wooded. Today the entire area surrounding the listed incline is heavily wooded, but with room enough for a delightful footpath to the top. The procedure for operations of the incline was one loaded wagon of five tons capacity of iron ore at the top which, when lowered under control of a brakesman, hauled up the several empty wagons attached to the rope on the other track. This procedure took about 12 minutes. To accomplish this task an engine house was built at the top of the incline and recessed into the ground so that the two rail tracks ran across the top before merging and continuing to Gupworthy. Inside were two iron rope-winding drums 18ft (5.5m) in diameter and 3¼ft (3.25m) in width. In later years the power source for the winding engine was converted to a Robey steam engine.

At the head of the incline there grew up a small community which had a shop, chapel and workshops

This close view of a disc and crossbar signal varied between the different railway companies, but normally the disc and bar were set at 90° to each other so that the bar facing the oncoming train indicated stop. When rotated 90° so that the disc faced the oncoming train, it indicated line clear. However, signalling was never really a problem on the WSMR, as there was normally only one train in steam.

An example of the
Neilson 0-4-0ST
locomotives used
on the WSMR.
This locomotive
Newport was built
in 1855, rebuilt
in 1895 and
photographed
here in 1896.
It was used as
a temporary
replacement on the
WSMR in 1896.

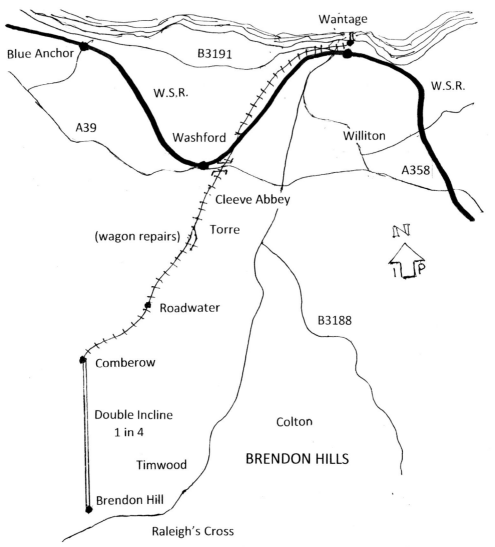

with rail lines spreading out in both directions to the several iron ore mines. In the period of the mid-1870s mineral production was around 40,000 tons per annum, including imported coal which amount, by the peak of 1877, to over 52,000 tons. During the heyday of the mineral railway, passengers were carried on the lower sections with four trains a day although they did ride up the incline in the empty wagons at their own risk. The records show that in around 1875 there were just over 300 miners diminishing to around 87 in 1883.

Steam locomotives that worked on the Somerset mineral railway included a very basic 'square box' tank of the loco built by Neilson, an 0-4-0ST in 1856; there was of course no

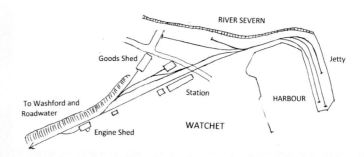

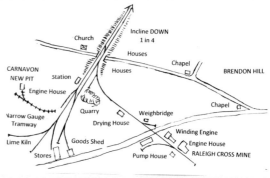

cab protection at all. The first loco was used in the construction of the line with two more Neilsons that worked the upper levels to the mines. Sharp Stewart provided 0-6-0ST tanks named *Rowcliffe* and *Brendon* built in 1857. Another two from the same manufacturer named *Pontypool* and *Atlas* were supplied by the Ebbw Vale Company for passenger

An early photograph after the closure of the railway looking down the incline in the early 1940s before nature completely took over the line.

A level crossing keeper's hut showing evidence of the old track bed where it crossed Torre Road in the hamlet of Faircross, near Torre Rocks village, just past the White Horse Inn. The next station going in the direction of Combe Row would have been Roadwater. 2019

traffic in February 1865. Passenger coaches of four wheels were supplied by the Welsh iron founders company.

Some early wagons delivered were used in the construction of the railway with a few suffering damage. In the early 1860s there were 32 wagons rising to 116 over the next 15 years. All open wagons were low sided with a payload of only five tons because of the incline restrictions. A later introduction with some degree of 'class' was the former London Metropolitan Railway condensing tank engine, No.37, a 4-4-0T purchased second hand in June 1907 that was later sold to the GWR.

The mine finally closed in 1923 following cheaper prices of imported iron ore from around the world, which was the death knell to the mines in the Brendon Hills. The property,

A short road tunnel running under the old track bed of the WSMR near Combe Row station before the base of the incline. 2019

This photo shows the remains of the old winding house for the Brendon incline. It housed two large winding drums approximately 18ft (5.5m) in diameter and 3¼ft (1m) wide mounted on frames and secured to the floor. The two incline cables were 1,000ft (305m) in length and worked on the self-acting principle relying on the heavier load descending and pulling up the lighter wagons. In later years a small steam engine was installed to turn the drums.

track and several cottages were sold at auction on August 8, 1924, which was a sad day for all the small communities along its route.

Today, many signs of this old mineral railway are still very evident and provide an entrancing and delightful walk in the wooded hills and valley.

West Somerset Railway

The county of Somerset today is a tourist and holiday hotspot with coastal towns and villages such as Weston-super-Mare, Burnham-on-Sea, Watchet, Blue Anchor and Minehead all accessible by road. The only national rail link runs from Bristol Temple Meads to Weston-super-Mare then inland to Taunton and down to Exeter with no service to these

other coastal towns. This was not always the case.

By 1844 the Bristol and Exeter Railway (B&ER) had fully opened. Its engineer was Isambard Kingdom Brunel, so the line was built as 7ft ¼in (2,140mm) broad gauge for a seamless operation with his Great Western Railway (GWR).

The nearest B&ER station to these coastal towns was Taunton and an Act of Parliament dated August 17, 1857 authorised the newly incorporated West Somerset Railway to build a broad gauge line form Taunton to Watchet. The engineer was George Furness of London. Construction started on April 7, 1859, with work commencing at Crowcombe, a little over half way from Taunton and took nearly three years to complete the two-

The 13.50 train from Taunton approaches Williton on April 25, 1960 making its way towards Minehead headed up by a Class 4575 2-6-2T No. 5554, built at GWR Swindon Works on November 30, 1928 and withdrawn on August 31, 1963 after 35 years' service.

mile (3.2km) line. The first passenger train arrived at Watchet on March 31, 1862 with goods traffic starting in the following August.

A further Act of Parliament passed on June 29, 1871 was for building an extension in broad gauge from the West Somerset Railway at Watchet to Minehead. Construction started in 1872 and the line was finally opened on July 16, 1874 giving a total track length from Taunton to Minehead of 22¾ miles (36.4km). On January 1, 1876 the B&ER was amalgamated into Brunel's GWR and following the 'gauge wars' these lines were converted to standard gauge in 1882.

As holiday traffic increased to the Somerset coast and Exmoor, passing loops were installed

A 1955 photo of a GWR, Churchward, Class 4300, 2-6-0 No.5306, built at GWR Swindon Works in 1917 and useful for mixed traffic. It is seen here on the turntable at Minehead being pointed in the right direction for its return journey to Taunton and was finally withdrawn on July 31, 1964.

A view at Minehead station in 1960 with a 2-6-2T Class 4575, No. 5571 standing idle and were often referred to as the 'small prairie class'. It was built in 1929 at the GWR Swindon Works and withdrawn in 1964. The goods shed is shown behind the loco.

and improvements made to stations. From Minehead the stations are Dunster, Blue Anchor, Washford, Watchet, Doniford Halt, Williton, Stogumber, Crowcombe, Bishops Lydeard, Norton Fitzwarren and Taunton. Under the Railways Act of 1921 the West Somerset Railway was amalgamated into the GWR empire. Realising the needs of holidaymakers who found hotels

out of their financial reach, camping coaches were situated in sidings at Blue Anchor and Stogumber stations so that people could enjoy the local countryside or hop on a train to a nearby coastal resort.

Although the amenities continued to grow and improve in these resorts, including the 1962 opening of Butlin's Holiday Camp in Minehead, the line did

Williton station opened on March 31, 1862 for broad gauge track that was then used by the West Somerset Railway and became a part of Great Western Railway in 1876 and converted to standard gauge in 1882. The GWR footbridge was installed in 2011 and was originally from Trowbridge, as the original was removed by BR in the 1960s. This photo was taken in 2020 after the first Covid-19 lockdown and was eerily quiet.

BRCW Type 3 No. 6566 or as they became, Class 33/0 No. 33048 Bo-Bo diesel electric, one of 98 built by Birmingham Railway Carriage and Wagon Co. for BR Southern Region between 1960 and 1962 and often referred to as 'Cromptons' because of the Crompton Parkinson electrical equipment installed in them. They had a maximum speed of 85mph (136kph). It was withdrawn from BR service in 1995 and started work at WSR in 1997.

not produce sufficient revenue and was recommended for closure in Beeching's Reshaping of British Railways Report in 1963. Despite continuing to make a loss it remained in operation thanks to a programme of gradually cutting out and shutting down whatever it could. It was finally closed on Saturday, January 2, 1971.

Following closure it was maintained for five years in a condition to restart operations should the need arise. Closure also sparked off negotiations by the Preservation Society and in May 1971 a new West Somerset Railway Company (WSRC) was formed with a view to operating a commuter service between Minehead and Taunton, but that never materialised. However, Somerset County Council bought the line from BR in 1973 and

An Andrew Barclay 0-4-0 diesel hydraulic locomotive No. 578 built in 1962 for the Royal Ordnance Factory at Puriton, near Bridgewater, in Somerset and was one of a pair along with 579. Both have been on WSR since 1991.

The Somerset and Dorset Railway Trust had a museum at Washford station, which is now permanently closed and also some railway stock, which has been moved away. This photo, taken before closure, shows their Ruston & Hornsby four-wheel diesel-mechanical loco No. 210479, built in 1942 for the Air Ministry, then to Cadbury's and finally to Bath Gasworks. Coupled up is a LSWR ventilated van and a LSWR brake van built around 1902and rebuilt in the 1990s by the SDRT.

GWR Class 7800, 4-6-0, *Odney Manor*, No.7828 is a Manor Class locomotive built at BR Swindon Works in 1950 and was withdrawn in 1965 and sent for scrap. It was saved from Barry scrapyard by a private buyer and after a chequered period was moved to the WSR in 1995 having been restored and was eventually sold to the WSR in 2004. It is seen here in 2019 approaching Watchet station.

leased it back to the WSRC and it gradually reopened as a heritage railway. Various efforts have been made since then to run regular services but nothing permanent has materialised.

The connection from Bishops Lydeard to Taunton was severed owing to objections from the local bus companies who thought that the railway would take away their business. A short head-shunt

was then provided at Bishops Lydeard for engines to run-round their passenger coaches. This has left Bishops Lydeard and Minehead as the two termini and a new turntable was installed at Minehead in 2008 to provide some operational flexibility.

The ethos of the West Somerset Railway is that the line should be as true as possible to the former GWR standards and

especially overall appearance, which has certainly been achieved. The WSR is Britain's longest heritage railway at 19.75 miles (31.6km). Rolling stock includes characterful freight wagons and coaches and diesel multiple units, diesel and GWR steam locomotives. As with many heritage railways, locomotives are regularly exchanged with other railways to ensure that there is always a changing scene of new items to enjoy.

Bishops Lydeard station, which is the inland terminus of the WSR viewed from the footbridge with GWR *Odney Manor*, No. 7828 and its six coaches having just arrived from Minehead in June 2019.

Immaculate! '4900' 'Hall' Class No 4936 *Kinlet Hall* stands at Minehead gently simmering away before taking the run up to Bishops Lydeard with an afternoon working during the Spring Gala in March 2009.
Peter Rowlands

The Railways of Yorkshire

From the 1830s and through the 1840s, the years of 'Railway Mania', Yorkshire benefited from the growth of the railways, dominated mainly by George Hudson, the 'Railway King'. The west side of Yorkshire saw most of the small companies operated by and then taken over by the London & North Western Railway and the Midland Railway. This became the London Midland & Scottish Railway (LMS) in 1923 at the time of the Railways Act that brought all the railway companies into the four groups of LMS, LNER, SR and GWR.

On the east side, the lines ended up being operated and owned by the North Eastern Railway and Great Northern Railway to become the London & North Eastern Railway (LNER) in 1923.

A few of these railways have been selected, including current, closed and maybe forgotten lines, and those that have risen again as heritage lines.

York railway station, 25 June 2019

This station in North Yorkshire is on the East Coast Main Line 189.6 miles (303.4km) from London King's Cross and operated by the new London & North Eastern Railway (LNER); a completely different type of operation from the steam days of the old LNER.

The original station was opened in 1839 by the York and North Midland Railway, owned by George Hudson, and was located outside the city walls, but was replaced in 1841 by a station built within the city walls. This was then replaced by the current station, opened on June 25, 1877, once more outside the city walls to accommodate through trains so that they did not have to reverse out, as was the case at the previous terminus.

A TransPennine Class 68, 68032, *Destroyer* built in 2017 by Stadler at their Valencia plant in Spain. It is seen here on a maintenance siding next to platform 2 awaiting any emergency duties required.

A view along platform 3 (platform 2 is to the left) looking south and amply shows the curve of the iron and glass canopy.

The new station started with 13 platforms and was the largest station in the world at that time. It has, of course, the impressive large curved, glass iron canopy (not over platforms 9, 10, & 11) and the footbridge that was added in 1938. Various changes have taken place over the years to the platforms, tracks, signalling etc., but the station remains fundamentally unchanged.

Currently, the platforms are 1 to 11 where 1, 2, 6, 7 and 8 are bay platforms. Platforms 3 and 4 are the same platform with 3 being the south end, 4 being the north and signalled bi-directionally. Platform 5 is also signalled bi-directionally with 5a and 5b.

An LNER Class 91 electric locomotive 91127 standing at platform 3 ready to continue its journey south from Edinburgh Waverley station to London Kings Cross. A total of 31 units were manufactured by British Rail Engineering Ltd (BREL) at Crewe Works from a design by GEC. They have top speed of 140mph (224kph) and 91127 was built in October 1990, so after 29 years' service they are being replaced by Hitachi Class 802 EMUs.

In platform 8 stands a Northern Class 170, two-car DMU, No. 170125 shortly to leave for Burley Park, near Leeds, from the north facing end of the station via the non-electrified Harrogate line. The Class 170 Turbostar was built by Bombardier Transportation in 1998 and this was one of 16 units cascaded down from Abelio Scotrail at end of 2018.

Waiting at platform 5 facing north is a new IET (Intercity Express Train), a Class 802 number 802 204 of TransPennine Express in works grey and as yet unbranded. They will be known as Nova 1. Manufactured by Hitachi of Japan, they are five-car sets of bi-mode operation, obtaining power from 25kV AC overhead catenary system of from diesel power. This unit had arrived from Manchester Airport after a test run. A total of 19 units have been ordered for TransPennine Express.

Platforms 9, 10 and 11 are also bi-directional. All tracks, except the track in bay platform 2 are electrified to the standard 25Kv ac 50Hz catenary system carried out in 1989. Platform 2 is for terminating trains on the non-electrified York to Scarborough Line and immediately branches to the right towards Malton.

Tracks coming into the south of the station are from the London, Doncaster, Leeds, Hull and Blackpool directions and those exiting north to Newcastle, Edinburgh, Scarborough and Harrogate, which branches left a short distance from the station and is a non-electrified line.

Train operators using the

station are LNER, Northern, TransPennine, Grand Central, Cross Country and East Midlands (weekends only). Destinations from York include Harrogate, Hull, Manchester Airport, Edinburgh, London King's Cross, Newcastle, Liverpool Lime Street, Blackpool North, Sunderland, Leeds,

Penzance, Inverness, Sheffield, Middlesbrough, Scarborough and Reading to name but a few. On this particular day the station was 142 years old!

Waiting at platform 10 to return to King's Cross is a new Class 800 No. 800 103 of LNER, known as an AZUMA (Japanese for 'East'). It is another version of the Hitachi IET range and entered service in May 2019 on the East Coast Main Line from London King's Cross to Edinburgh, Waverley. It has the bi-mode capability obtaining power from overhead catenary system and by diesel when required. LNER has ordered 13 sets of nine cars and 10 sets of five cars. Maximum speed is 140mph (224kph) using ETCS in-cab signalling.

Arriving at platform 9 is a Cross Country Class 220 No. 220 025 on route to Glasgow Central. Cross Country have 34 of these four-car DMU sets originally made by Bombardier at their Bruges, Belgium facility during 2000/2001. They are capable of 125mph (200kph).

At platform 3 is TransPennine Express
DMU Class 185 No.185 146 for
Scarborough. Class 185s are three-car sets
built by Siemens in Germany and first
introduced in 2006. TPE have 51 Class 185
sets. A refurbishment programme was put
into place in 2017 and completed in 2018.

A Northern Class 158 (Sprinter) DMU
No. 158 755 stands in platform 6 shortly to
leave for Blackpool North from the south
end of the station.
Northern have both
two- and three-car
sets, all of which
were built by British
Rail Engineering
Ltd (BREL) Derby
between 1989 and
1992.

York – Beverley Line

The standard gauge, York to Beverley Line in the East Riding of
Yorkshire was opened to Market Weighton on October 4, 1847 by
the York and North Midland Railway. The chairman of the Y&NMR
was of course George Hudson. The double track line left the York-
Scarborough line at Bootham Junction and ran southeast towards
Market Weighton, a distance of 21½ miles (34.5km). Hudson had
Londesborough halt built for his own private use as he bought the

A Northern Class 142 (Pacer) No.142 005 DMU arrived at the bay platform 2. These two-car units were built between 1985 and 87 by BREL using the design of a British Leyland bus. Northern had 79 of these units, which are now being phased out.

Now where did I leave my bicycle?

York Station in all its grandeur, enlivened by the appearance of the last steam locomotive to be built at Swindon, the 2-10-0, *Evening Star*, built for the last days of the 1960s.

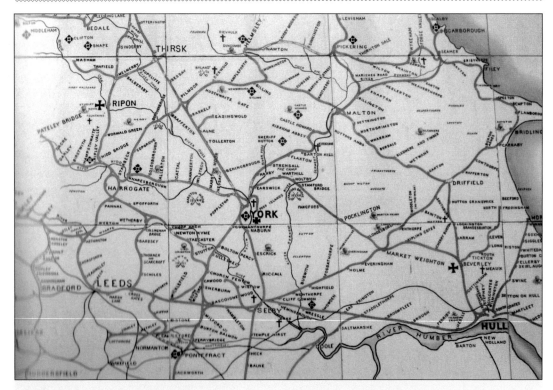

Pocklington station during 2019 clearly shows the roof of the train shed. The front of the station is used by East Yorkshire Bus Company as a drop off and pickup point as the bus depot is just opposite.

Londesborough Estate, giving him all the trappings of a successful business man. Unfortunately, the remaining line to Beverley was delayed as shares in Hudson's railway projects plummeted and investors lost their

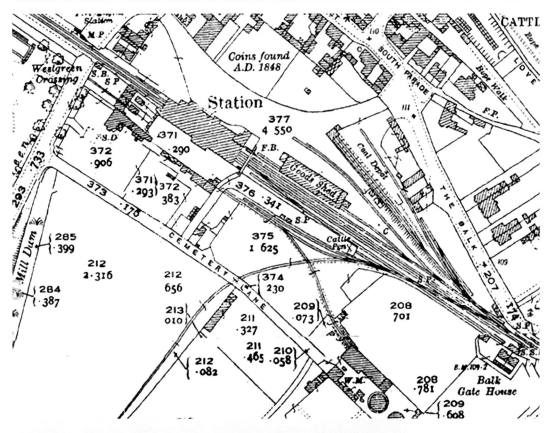

money because of his sharp business practices. He ended up bankrupt and died almost penniless in 1871.

It was 17 years before the remaining 11 miles (18km) of line were completed to Beverley by North Eastern Railway that had then taken over the line in 1854. Just outside Beverley the line joined the Hull to Scarborough route for the short run into Beverley. The Market Weighton to Beverley line was open for

Pocklington station end view; the front is to the left. The supporting pillars for the train shed roof can be clearly seen and are the same at the other end. The station is now owned by Pocklington School who use it but also it is a venue for various activities. The school shield is on the front of the doors.

traffic in 1865. There were 10 stations between York and Market Weighton and two between Market Weighton and Beverley, which was single track with passing loop at Kiplingcotes station.

The two main stations were Pocklington and Market Weighton, both of which had two platforms under an overall hipped roof train shed. The station buildings were single storey

and situated parallel to the platforms. Market Weighton had a two-road engine shed and turntable.

The only bridge of note is the Stamford Bridge Viaduct that crosses the River Derwent. It is still in place and consists of 24 arches and a 90ft (27.4m) cast iron span over the river. Also, three small bridges straddled cuttings along the rest of the line. There were 16 level-crossings

The railway bridge and viaduct at Stamford Bridge that crosses the River Derwent. It has a 90ft (27m) cast iron span over the river with 10 brick arches on the southeast side and five on the northwest. The span weighs over 260 tons.

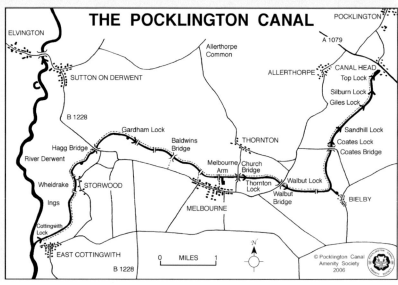

This photo shows Pocklington station, probably in the 1930s and shows the covered station shed and the footbridge at the far end. The goods shed is past the footbridge on the left and is still standing today.

The last train from Beverley to York seen here at Pocklington on November 27, 1965. It was hauled by a Thomson Class B1, 4-6-0 No. 61306 built by North British in April 1948. It was withdrawn in September 1967.

with three crossings around the Pocklington station area.

On January 1, 1923 the Railways Act saw the line brought under control of the London North Eastern Railway (LNER). By 1939 and the commencement of the Second World War, services were reduced and the odd station started to close. By the end of the war the damage caused by the Luftwaffe and lack of regular maintenance on rolling stock and rail infrastructure was evident. The railways were badly in need of investment and updating that could not be afforded by the Big Four, resulting in the nationalisation of 1948 and the formation of British Railways.

In the late 50s diesels were being evaluated as the replacement for steam and in 1957 some diesel multiple units (DMUs) started to appear on the York-Beverley line and took over regular duties. During 1959 three more stations closed and the line was earmarked for closure by Beeching. Services ended on November 27, 1965. At the time of closure only six of the 13 stations were still open. The 13 stations in order from York were: Earswick, Warthill, Holtby, Stamford Bridge, Fangfoss, Yapham Gate, Pocklington, Nunburnholme, Londesborough Park, Londesborough, Market Weighton, Kiplingcotes & Cherry Burton.

Incidentally, Pocklington also had its own canal that was built in 1818, was 9½ miles (15km) in length and ran down to the River Derwent at Cottingwith utilising nine locks. Barges carried coal, lime, fertilizer and industrial goods to Pocklington and agricultural products were carried out to the West Riding of Yorkshire. As these were all goods that Hudson's railways wanted to carry, the Y&NMR bought

A view through Market Weighton station in the snow. You will see it has a similar station shed to Pocklington. It was demolished in 1967 following the Beeching Axe that closed the line.

the canal and left it to decay. It was closed completely in 1934.

Local volunteer groups are now restoring stretches of the canal, resulting in five navigable miles (8km) and three working locks.

Rowntree's & York & Derwent Valley Light Railway

The 1¾-mile (2.8km) Foss Island freight line was opened in 1880 and branched off the North Eastern Railway York-to-Scarborough line just outside York. It served the York

In contrast this is Market Weighton station in 1964 where the station roof had been removed in 1947 and replaced with platform awnings. In the station is a BR Cravens Ltd, Class 105 two-car diesel-mechanical multiple unit of unknown serial number, built between 1956 and 1959. They were all withdrawn by end of 1988.

Gas Company, York Corporation power station, a warehouse and of course Rowntree's confectionary factory on Haxby Road that has become a household name with its products including Fruit Gums, Fruit Pastilles, Jelly Tots, Kit-Kat, Polo mints and so on.

A spur from the branch entered the factory area for the delivery of commodities for making the confectionary and to transport out the various finished products.

Rowntree's had their own steam locomotives that worked within their 1½-mile (2.4km) network, the first being delivered in 1890; a second hand 0-4-0T locomotive named *Marshall*. Four other steam 0-4-0T locomotives, three Hunslets and one Barclay, were bought between 1904 and 1943, but by 1959 steam was abandoned for three Ruston & Hornsby 0-4-0 diesels and in 1979 a Thomas Hill 0-6-0DH was added.

During 1927, as the factory developed and staff numbers increased, a station halt was built for the employees adjacent to the factory called Rowntree Halt and located on the Foss Islands branch. This was not an advertised service and was strictly for employees, who found it useful when travelling from Selby, Doncaster and areas south of York.

Rowntree's Ruston & Hornsby locomotive No.1 is an 0-4-0 Class 165DE, works number 423661 built in 1958 at the R&H Lincoln plant. It was donated to the Kent and East Sussex Railway in 1987 and is resplendent in Rowntree's green livery. It normally provides piloting services around Rolvenden yard.

This is Rowntree's locomotive No.2 seen here at the Derwent Valley Light Railway (DVLR) yard at Murton awaiting restoration. It is a Ruston & Hornsby 0-4-0 Class 88DS, works number 421419 built in 1959. It was later transferred to Rowntree's Fawden Works near Newcastle and was then transferred to the North Yorkshire Moors Railway (NYMR) in 1987 along with No.3 for preservation. It was moved to the DVLR in 2015 for restoration which is ongoing.

Rowntree's locomotive No.3 is a Ruston & Hornsby 0-4-0 Class 88DS, works number 432479 built in 1959. It was transferred to Rowntree's Fawdon Works near Newcastle in 1980, but was surplus to requirements by 1987 and was taken to the NYMR for preservation. By 2006 it was at the National Railway Museum at Shildon and finally moved to the DVLR at Murton in 2013 where it has been beautifully restored by Glynnis and Tony Frith.

After a major track reorganisation in the factory area in 1972, British Railway Registration Plates were removed from the locomotives confining their operations to within the factory area. The extra track required was purchased second-hand from the Darlington Railway Plant and Foundry Co. and laid by existing Rowntree staff.

A majority of Rowntree's confectionary products left the factory by British Rail owned VDA box vans with painted white roofs that reflected the sun in hot weather to prevent heat damage to the chocolate cargo.

Rowntree's sold out to the Swiss company Nestle in 1988, and following reorganisation Rowntree Halt was officially

A Thomas Hill 0-6-0 DH works number 285V built 1979 seen here as Rowntree's No.4 at York station, September 7, 1981. It is painted yellow with striking red Rowntree-Mackintosh logo on the side.

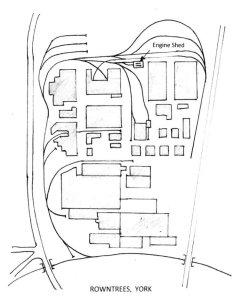

ROWNTREES, YORK

A view from 1985 looking down the branch with Rowntree's factory and Rowntree Halt to the left. A BR Class 08 is running round, having assembled a rake of BR VDA vans with their white roofs that reflect the sun and assist in keeping the chocolate products in good condition during transit. The spur into the factory is a little further down the line, on the left, past the Halt.

closed on July 8, 1989 although Rowntree's carried on using the Foss Islands branch until final closure later that year with track being lifted in 1992.

Fortunately, the three Ruston & Hornsby locomotives have been rescued for preservation; Ruston & Hornsby 0-4-0 165DE, No.1 (works number 423661/1958) has been restored to a working condition at the Kent and East Sussex Heritage Railway.
Ruston & Hornsby 0-4-0 88DS, No.2 (works number 421419/1958) is currently being restored by the Derwent Valley Light Railway (DVLR) near York.
Ruston & Hornsby 0-4-0 88DS, No.3 (works number 432479/1959) has been restored to a working condition at the DVLR.
The Thomas Hill 0-6-0DH, No.4 (works number 285V/1979) was relocated to Total Oil, Immingham and is now known to be at Lindsey Oil Refinery in Lincolnshire and named *Tigga*. Rowntree's No.3 was transferred to the new Rowntree's Fawdon Works near Newcastle in the late 1950s.

Derwent Valley Light Railway

The privately owned Derwent Valley Light Railway was originally built as standard gauge line and opened fully in 1913. As a 'light' railway, speed was limited to 25mph (40.2kph), which would benefit the use of level crossings, many with no gates and just cattle grids. They were mainly single track with lighter rails and signalling was minimal or non-existent with usually one engine in steam. Colonel Stephens was a great advocate of the light railway.

The DVLR diverted from the Foss Islands branch, just past Rowntree's, and operated between Layerthorpe and Cliffe Common, which was at the junction of the Selby – Market Weighton – Driffield line, a total of

16 miles (26km). This was one of George Hudson's original railway lines opened in 1849 as the York and North Midland Railway and subsequently NE, and LNER and finally BR. The DVLR line boasted 11 stations with Layerthorpe station and goods yard being the first, just a short distance from the Foss Islands branch.

Layerthorpe station yard had a locomotive shed, water tank, goods warehouse, Shell-Mex oil depot and of course the station building and general manager's office. The other stations were Osbaldwick, Murton Lane, Dunnington Halt, Dunnington (for Kexby), Elvington, Wheldrake, Cottingwith, Thorganby and Skipwith. Most of the line was through rural areas and served the scattered villages along the

The DVLR bought two Ford-based railbuses, seen here coupled back to back and working as a single unit. Initially, they thought that they had to run a single units, and as a result had turntables installed at each end of the line to allow them to be driven forwards in both directions.

This shows a very rural line somewhat overtaken by nature with a typical short freight train on the Derwent Valley Light Railway during July 1964. The locomotive is a BR Class 03, 0-6-0, No. D2112 built around 1957. In the middle is a former SECR green brake van purchased from the Southern Railway in 1946.

This photo, again taken in 1964, shows D2112 and train at Wheldrake with the cement wagon having been decoupled on the adjacent grass covered siding. The building to the right is a Food Buffer Store built by the Ministry of Works in 1952 to store sugar, corned beef, flour etc. in case of nuclear attack, as this was during the Cold War.

A delightful scene at Dunnington station on the DVLR in 1979. With the opening of the National Railway Museum in York in 1975 the DVLR decided to run a 'Summer Steam Service' during the summers of 1977 and 1979 and purchased a J72, 0-6-0T locomotive named *Joem* for the purpose. It was built at the BR/LNER Darlington Works in 1951 and was withdrawn from service in 1962 and is now owned by North Eastern Locomotive Preservation Group and is kept at the North Yorkshire Moors Railway.

Derwent Valley. On reaching Cliff Common the DVLR ran into its own terminal platform parallel to the LNER platform with its own sidings and connections to the main line.

The DVLR was always a privately owned railway and was primarily a freight line and affectionately known as the 'The Blackberry Line', as in its heyday it transported blackberries to London's Covent Garden via York. Some passenger trains were introduced, but were withdrawn in 1926. The freight continued through the Second World War and struggled into the 1960s although services had reduced to one return journey each day. After BR closed the Selby/Driffield line in 1964, it left the DVLR going nowhere at its southern end, as it was quite a distance from Selby.

Even today, Cliff Common remains a very rural area and

would not benefit from any reopening of a DVLR railway terminus. Inevitably sections of line were then closed leaving only four miles (6½km) of track between Layerthorpe and Dunnington on the outskirts of York. The last train ran on September 27, 1981 although Rowntree's continued to use the Foss Islands branch until the branch was finally closed in 1989.

Locomotive types used over its lifetime were numerous with many being hired in although it purchased its own from 1969 onwards. In the early days it tried using a rail-lorry that did not meet expectations and then two railbuses that required turntables to be installed at Layerthorpe and Skipwith.

Today some of the old track is now foot and cycle paths, but around half a mile (0.8km) of track at Murton Park has been laid by the preservation group of the Derwent Valley Light Railway. They have a number of diesel locomotives and several carriages and an assortment of wagons. The privately owned and fully restored Rowntree's No.3 is kept at this site and ex Rowntree's No.2 is being restored by the DVLR.

Sand Hutton Light Railway

Warthill, the second station from York on the Beverley line, was also an interchange for the Sand Hutton Light Railway owned by Sir Robert Walker to service his large estate in the Derwent Valley. The total length of the line was 5¼ miles (8.4km) and was a single track 18in (457mm) narrow gauge system completed by 1922 and converted from an existing 15in (381mm) miniature gauge railway.

It was not unknown for some large estates to have their own narrow gauge railways for the purpose of moving coal and general provisions apart from providing rides for the family.

Walker's 15in (381mm) miniature railway ran from the outskirts of Sand Hutton village and through the Sand Hutton Hall estate and was established in 1910. One of the locomotives was a 4-4-2 built for the Sand Hutton estate by Bassett-Lowke in Northampton and named Synolda after Sir Robert's wife. Following the First World War, Walker obtained another Light Railway Order to extend the 15in (381mm) line to 7¾ miles (12.4km) to link up with the North Easter

A branch from the running line went to Claxton Brickworks and this view shows an unknown 0-4-0WT with wooden trucks probably loaded with coal for the brick furnaces.

Railway (NER) at Warthill station. However, as the line was nearing completion in 1920 it became clear that the rolling stock was not robust enough to carry the goods in and out of the estate.

Claxton brickworks on the estate required coal to be delivered and bricks to be transported away, plus produce from the farms on the estate, and not forgetting passengers.

A train headed up by an 0-4-0WT at Bossall station, albeit a garden shed and rough ground.

The engine shed with an unknown 0-4-0 WT and probably Sir Robert Walker at the entrance and the driver almost standing to attention!

This posed photo
is obviously Sir
Robert Walker
standing proudly
by his unknown
locomotive, which
may have been
Esme, named after
his second wife.
He purchased
this locomotive in
1927.

Not to be deterred, Sir Robert investigated
ways to upgrade his railway and in 1920 a
further light Railway order then allowed him
to convert the 15in (381mm) line to 18in
(457mm).

During December 1920, Sir Robert
purchased four locomotives from the
Deptford Meat Depot that became surplus
to requirements and shortly afterward the
extension to Warthill station was completed
with the required transfer sidings. By April
1922 the first 4¼ miles (6.8km) was opened
between Warthill station and the sidings at
Kissthorns, near the main hall, together with
an extension to Claxton brickworks. A further
extension to Bossall and Barnby House was
opened in 1923. Another extension across
the River Derwent to Scrayingham was also
authorised but never carried out owing to the
cost of building a bridge over the river. The

total length of the line was 5¼ miles (8.4km).

The line was in use by passengers until
1930 although the brickworks closed in 1929
and Sir Robert Walker died in 1930. The line
struggled on until closure in June 1932 and was
dismantled in 1933.

The locomotives were built by Hunslet and
were 0-4-0WT, numbered 4, 10, 11 and 12
with works number 1207, 1289, 1290 and 1291
respectively. The first locomotive to be bought
was No.4 in 1916, the rest in 1917.

There were a total of 75 wooden wagons
built on four-wheel frames with drop sides and
dumb buffers. The passengers were catered for
by a coach, built in 1924 by Robert Hudson of
Leeds and seated 30 persons together with a
private saloon area for the Walker family. The
coach had the benefit of electric lighting and
vacuum brakes.

This shows off the
passenger coach
with the guard
standing upright
with Sir Robert
Walker.

North Yorkshire Moors Railway (NYMR)

The NYMR is a preserved standard gauge line, mainly using steam locomotives and runs north from Pickering across the North Yorkshire Moors to Whitby on the Yorkshire east coast, a distance of 18 miles (29km). From the line's conception to the 21st century it has had several owners;

Whitby & Pickering Railway (W&PR)	1836-1845
York & North Midland Railway (Y&NMR)	1845-1854
North Eastern Railway (NER)	1854-1922
London North Eastern Railway (LNER)	1923-1947
British Railways (BR)	1948-1965
North Yorkshire Moors Railway (NYMR) (preservation)	1967 onwards

This George Stephenson railway started life in 1835 when it opened between Whitby and Grosmont and then south to Pickering in 1836 using a rope worked incline to raise the line from the River Esk Valley. In 1845 the railway was bought by the York and North Midland Railway (Y&NMR) that was part of George Hudson's railway empire. Hudson reengineered the line for steam locomotives and re-equipped the incline with stationary steam locomotives.

A view looking towards the buffer stops at Pickering Station that has all the trappings of a station of its time with bookshop, tea room, toilets and a WHSmith paper stall. The link to Rillington Junction originally continued on past the buffer stops. Note the recent station roof built in 2007.

Ex BR 4MT
2-6-0 No. 76079
departs Pickering
with the 12.00
train for Whitby
with the next
station, Levisham,
six miles through
fairly wooded
countryside.
This locomotive
was designed by
Robert Riddles
and built at
Horwich Works,
Bolton, in
February 1957.
It had a short life
of 10 years and
was withdrawn
in June 1967,
taken to Barry
scrapyard where
it was rescued for
preservation.

Levisham station
reopened for
business in 1973,
but was far from
the idyllic country
station that you
see today: track
was missing, only
one platform could
be used, signalling
was out of action
and the level
crossing only had
a couple of farm
gates and that was
just for starters!
Since then the
station has been
transformed with
a fully operational
signal box, full
barrier crossing,
sidings and a
proper station
masters garden.

The line was extended south
from Pickering to a junction
at Rillington (near Malton) on
the York to Scarborough Line.
In 1854 the Y&NMR became
a part of the North Eastern
Railway (NER) who made many
improvements and made use
of the technical advancements,
installing block signalling, signal
cabins and a larger 45ft (13.7m)
turntable for the longer more
powerful locomotives. The NER
also constructed a new route to
bypass the incline and allowed
trains to be steam hauled from
Pickering to Grosmont.

As a result of the Railway
Act, the line became a part
of London & North Eastern

Arriving at Levisham station is a short train hauled by a J27, 0-6-0, No. 65894 designed by Worsdell. Built at Darlington Works in September 1923 for North Eastern Railway (NER) it was numbered 2392 and was taken out of service in September 1967. Its last shed was 54A, Sunderland South Dock. On its arrival, an exchange of tokens is taking place to ensure safe onward travel to Pickering.

Railway (LNER) in 1923, but little changed. It endured the Second World War during which, like all our railways, it gradually lacked the necessary maintenance since all effort went into serving the war effort. The line was nationalised in 1948 and absorbed into British Railways (BR). In 1952 Pickering station lost its

overall roof as it was deemed unsafe. The line's death knell came with the Beeching Report and it was subsequently closed down to Rillington Junction to passengers on March 6, 1965 and good trains in 1966.

However, Whitby to Grosmont formed a part of the line that branched from

Readying to pull away from Goathland in the Levisham direction is the BR 4MT No. 76067 with a train of ex BR coaches in the maroon livery of that era. The first coach, SC16191, is a composite corridor type, built at BR Works Derby in 1961. Note the workshop with water tank above and the water tower with its cylindrical upright column and swan neck water spout, both of which are circa 1865.

The lower quadrant signal is clear and the J27, No. 65894, tender first, starts to move out of Goathland station towards Grosmont. Just before the head shunt is the point to switch back into the single track and can be clearly seen 100yds (91m) past the platform.

Grosmont across to Middlesbrough and was also listed for closure, but was subsequently reprieved and now forms the Esk Valley Line. The 36-mile (58km) Esk Valley Railway is a non-profit community rail partnership started in 2005 and funded mainly by Northern Rail and North Yorkshire County Council for the benefit of local residents and visitors. At the time of writing, its daily timetable had five trains in each direction with a journey time of 90 minutes.

In 1967, the NYMR Preservation Society was formed and eventually became the NYM Historical Railway Trust in 1972. Initially, trains had to terminate at Grosmont, as NYMR was not licensed to run over Network Rail metals to Whitby, but since 2007 that has now changed and many trains run the full distance from Pickering to Whitby.

There are three stations between Pickering and Whitby, namely Levisham, Goathland and Grosmont. They are all situated in attractive

At Grosmont the Class S15, 4-6-0 No. 825 is just leaving with its train to Pickering. Originally designed for the LSWR by Robert Urie, the class was used extensively when absorbed into Southern Railway and was modified by Richard Maunsell. It was built at Eastleigh in 1927.

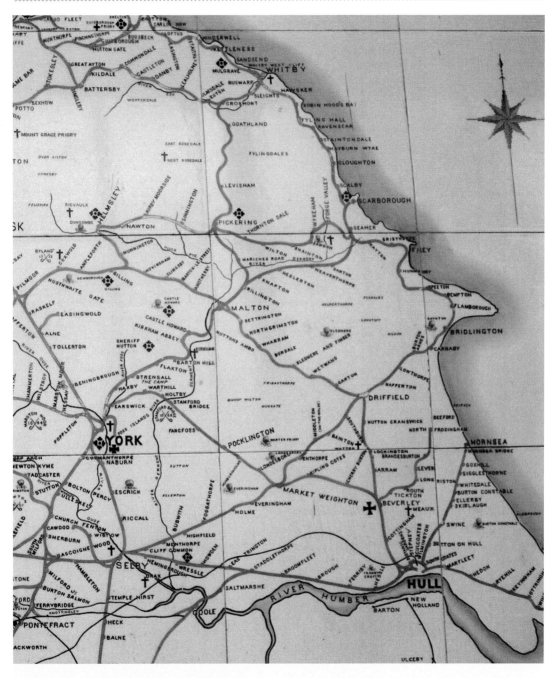

rural areas with Levisham in particular way out in the Newton Dale valley being nearly two miles down a steep, single track lane from the attractive Levisham village.

After much renovation, rebuilding and a new overall roof replaced in 2011, the NYMR now runs a very successful timetable of mainly steam-hauled trains. It also enjoys fame on television allowing the public to see and understand the organisation and hard work that goes on behind the scenes to keep the railway running.

A standard BR Class 9F, a 2-10-0 No. 92134, was designed by Robert Riddles and built at Crewe Works in 1957. This class of very powerful locomotives were the last standard class locomotives to be built in the UK. It is seen here at Grosmont running round to take its train back to Pickering.

Running round at Whitby station is 'Black Five' LMS Class 5, 4-6-0, No. 45428 named in preservation as *Eric Treacy*. Designed by William Stanier and built in Newcastle it entered service in October 1937 and worked for 30 years. Eric Treacy was the Bishop of Wakefield, well known for his railway photography. The station is shared with the NR Esk Valley line that runs between Whitby and Middlesborough and is operated by Northern Trains.

Settle to Carlisle Line

The Settle to Carlisle line (S&C), opened for freight in 1865 and passenger traffic in 1876, has become an iconic route from Settle, in North Yorkshire, crossing the remote, scenic areas of the Yorkshire Dales and the North Pennines to Carlisle Citadel station on the border with Scotland and onward to Glasgow and Edinburgh. The decision to build the line was made to overcome problems the Midland

Railway (MR) continually had with the London and North Western Railway (LNWR) over access rights to jointly run on their lines in Scotland.

The 73-mile (117km), standard gauge, double track line was constructed for the Midland Railway (MR) by more than 6,000 navvies and managed by their engineer John Crossley. It was no easy task and required 14 tunnels and 22 viaducts with the summit at Ais Gill being 1,169ft (356m) above sea level. The line was engineered to express standards

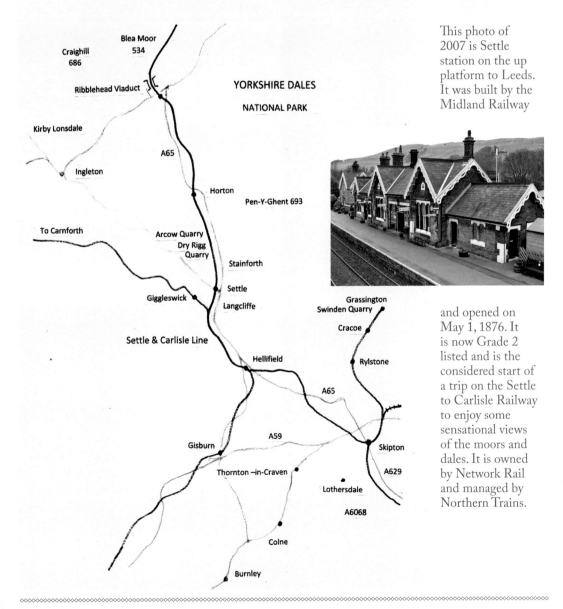

This photo of 2007 is Settle station on the up platform to Leeds. It was built by the Midland Railway and opened on May 1, 1876. It is now Grade 2 listed and is the considered start of a trip on the Settle to Carlisle Railway to enjoy some sensational views of the moors and dales. It is owned by Network Rail and managed by Northern Trains.

The date of this photo is November 12, 1935 and shows the LMS 'Thames Forth' train heading through the North Yorkshire moors on its way to Carlisle and Edinburgh Waverley. The locomotive is Jubilee Class 4-6-0 No. 5568 *Western Australia*, built in 1934 by North British Locomotive Company (NBR) in Glasgow to Stanier design. Note the box van behind the tender. It is a NBR fruit and yeast van with automatic vacuum brake (AVB) and through steam heat piping.

throughout its length with little thought given to any local traffic, although local stations/halts were built.

The outstanding viaduct on the line is the 24-arch Ribblehead Viaduct, which is 104ft (32m) high and 440yds (402m) in length. Shortly after, the line enters Blea Moor tunnel being

2,629yds (2,404m) long and running 500ft (152m) below the moor. As a requirement to enable the steam locomotives to keep good time and not lose speed, water troughs measuring 380yds (347m) in length and steam heated against severe winter weather were laid between the tracks at Garsdale.

Passenger trains leaving the MR London terminus of St Pancras were referred to as the 'Scotch Expresses' and by the early 20th century there were five daily trains, three to Glasgow and two to Edinburgh. Journey times were not as fast as those on the LNWR route but the MR prided itself on passenger comfort and good service. In the 1923 Big Four grouping, MR and LNWR found themselves merged together as part of London Midland and Scottish Railways (LMS) and any advantage that either company thought they had previously enjoyed was lost. From 1927 these trains were renamed 'Thames-Clyde' and 'Thames Forth' expresses, the

This is Dent, the highest station on the line at 1,150 ft (350m) above sea level. It is owned by Network Rail and managed by Northern. It was originally built by the Midland Railway and opened in 1877. Waiting at the platform is Northern service to Carlisle, a DMU Class 153, 153332, Super Sprinter built by British Rail Engineering from 1991. It is coupled to another two-car set.

The new 'Waverley' at Carlisle station during August 2011 with LMS Stanier 5MT, 4-6-0, Black Five at the front end. It was built at LMS Horwich Works and entered service in September 1945 and was withdrawn in August 1968. It is now in preservation and resides at West Coast Railways Motive Power Depot at Carnforth, Cumbria.

latter being eventually renamed 'The Waverley'.

By the 1950s, following nationalisation, British Railways (BR) started closing stations on the line, as the West Coast main line was being electrified and promising higher speeds, relegating the S&C to mainly freight services with trains being hauled by an assortment of ex LNER A3 Pacifics, BR standard Class 6 and 7 Pacifics and heavy duty 9F 2-10-0s. Then along came the Beeching Report!

In 1963 the Beeching Report into restructuring BR recommended withdrawal of all passenger services on the line and it was thought that it would

Settle Limes Co. Ltd at Horton Limeworks on a working day that is temporarily halted for the photograph. On the left is an Albion four-wheeled truck, circa 1930s and on the right a standard gauge 0-6-0ST locomotive believed to be Horton No.1.

A Gloucester Wagon and Carriage Co. 12 ton, four-plank, dropside wagon No.247, delivered to John Delaney in Horton-in-Ribbleside on May 24, 1929. It probably didn't look like that for long!

eventually be closed completely, but things limped along until the 1970s when it was then obvious that because of lack of investment the line and its infrastructure were deteriorating, especially the tunnels and viaducts and in particular the Ribblehead Viaduct. In 1984 closure notices were posted at the remaining stations; the result was outrage and the Friends of the S&C mounted a campaign to save the line because of its unique attraction to the tourist industry and for local use. The line was then reprieved by the government in April 1989 and work began with the renovation of stations and repair work to the viaducts and tunnels.

Today, Northern Trains runs passenger services from Leeds via Settle to Carlisle Citadel station and freight traffic is frequently using the line. It is also used as a diversionary route when the electrified West Coast mainline is closed for maintenance work, but trains have to be hauled by diesel locomotives. Last but not least there are railway touring companies that take their passengers by train from Leeds and York up the S&C normally hauled by BR Black 5 steam locomotives up to Carlisle. One company has nostalgically named their train 'The Waverley'!

The Settle and Carlisle is not just a rail line between centres, it serves some important commercial businesses along the route that have their own sidings. During the uncertain times for the line, companies turned to road transport, but the rough terrain of the moors and inadequate roads made the transport of quarried materials difficult for large vehicles. That situation is now in reverse.

A view of Horton Limeworks with wagon shunting in progress. To the right are the empty wagons waited to be loaded under the hopper, which is probably fed from the gantry to its right. Date unknown.

Horton Quarry

Freight mainly consisted of livestock during the early years, but some limestone quarries in the area were connected to the line by their own private sidings. The largest in the area was Horton Quarry located in Horton-in-Ribblesdale, eight miles (12.8km) north of Settle. It started business in 1888. By 1914 John Delaney, a coal merchant from Settle, had bought the company and acquired more land for future development. He purchased nine 10-ton wagons from the Midland Railway, bringing his fleet of private owner wagons to 1,009.

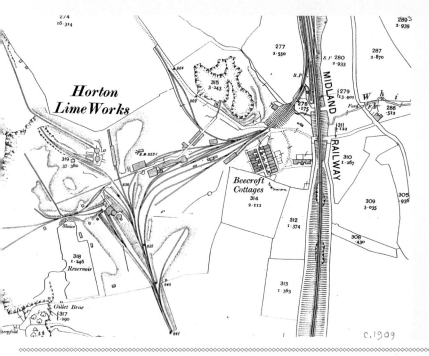

The 10 tonne VTG leased HYA bottom discharging bogie hopper wagons being filled with crushed aggregate by a bucket loader at the new Tarmac Arcow/Dry Rigg sidings. As the train is too long to fit along the loading platform, it is split into three lengths requiring the use of all three sidings. The train is coupled up after all train lengths have been loaded.

This evocative view shows the loaded train leaving the loading area and making its way down the short spur to the main line. The immediate area has been landscaped and planted with trees.

The operation required standard steam locomotives to carry out shunting duties on the three miles (4.8km) of internal sidings and became the largest quarry and lime works in the Dales. By 1936, Horton Quarry had purchased 50% of the Craven Lime Company and replaced Delaney's large fleet of wagons with Craven's own 2,500 wagons of which 1,600 were purchased from the MR.

To manage the uplift in business, the rail sidings were increased and several Manning Wardle tank locomotives were purchased similar to those used by the contractor who built the S&C. This extensive internal standard gauge railway system remained active into the mid-1970s when the steam locomotives were replaced by two Ruston & Hornsby 0-4-0 diesel locomotives, *Rayleigh* and *Ramsey*, built in 1952 and 1957 respectively.

Today, following changes of ownership over the years, the quarry is now owned by the Hanson Aggregate Group. The site has a stone crusher, several kilns fired by gas and produces around 600,000 tonnes of high quality lime, most of which is destined for cement manufacturers in the Manchester Area.

This unexpected photo was taken just as *Tornado*, the 2008 newly built LNER Peppercorn A1 No. 601631, came through with a day excursion train. The GB Railfeight Class 66 waits with its train to join the main line.

A spectacular view of GB Railfreight Class 66 No. 66752, *The Hoosier State*, hauling its Tarmac wagons over the Ribblehead viaduct. The Hoosier State is with reference to boatmen of Indiana, USA, who took corn or maize to New Orleans and is now a term applied to residents of the State!

This is a timber train coming from the north with an unknown Colas Rail Class 66 at the front and making its way through Garsdale station in 2019. The station was once known as Garsdale and Hawes Junction as a six mile (9.6km) branch line went to Hawes. The line was closed to passengers in March 1959 and to goods traffic in April 1964.

Although the company's own rail sidings have now been removed, the products are taken by road to the nearby transfer sidings adjacent to Ribblehead station, which are also used for transport by rail of locally felled timber. However, it is hoped that Hanson will renew sidings and a link to the S&C in the future.

Arcow and Dry Rigg Quarries

In order to remove heavy transport from the inadequate roads of the Yorkshire Dales National Park two quarries, Arcow and its near neighbour Dry Rigg, both owned by Tarmac,

The timber train runs through Garside station with its bogie bolster wagons loaded with cut lengths of timber, stacked and securely roped down between the uprights along each side.

have been reconnected by a new 750yd (685m) track from the S&C and ending in a siding fan at the loading end of the Arcow quarry. The new connection to the S&C is about 400yds (366m) north of the previous sidings, as they were found to be unsuitable. The last train left the original sidings in 1969 with the closure of the adjacent Helwith Bridge signal box with stone then being transported by road.

GB Railfreight Class 66s now leave five times every week with a rake of 16 ten tonne VTG leased HYA bottom discharging bogie hopper wagons destined for Hunslet East (Leeds), Agecroft (Manchester) and Bredbury

Approaches to the large Carlisle central station which served several railway companies, including the terminus of Scotland's premier line, The Caledonian. Here are two of their Drummond-designed locos with coaching stock being hauled out of the platforms.

A popular Black 5 Class 4-6-0 with its train of red liveried coaches in the hills and dales on the Settle and Carlisle line, approaching the summit of Ais Gill.

(Stockport). As the products from Arcow and Dry Rigg are slightly different they are loaded into separate wagons. This operation is estimated to save 16,000 road journeys every year.

Although not a local business, 2014 saw the start of a daily freight train of logs from Carlisle via the S&C to Chirk near Wrexham in Wales. The logs originate from south west Scotland where the trees are felled according to sustainable practices and sawn into shorter lengths for transportation by road to Carlisle.

At Carlisle yard they are then loaded onto KFA flatbed wagons with vertical bars to contain the logs and firmly strapped down. There are normally 15 wagons hauled by a Colas Rail Ltd Class 66 EMD diesel electric locomotive.

The logs are unloaded at Chirk for Kronospan Ltd an Austrian company manufacturing fibreboard, laminated flooring panels and other wood products for timber framed houses etc.

Thames-Clyde Express with BR standard Class 7, 4-6-2 appropriately named *Firth of Forth* making its way through the glorious countryside along the Settle and Carlisle line.

The Snailbeach District Railway

A view across the rolling Shropshire countryside from the long gone Snailbeach lead mines and narrow gauge railway up in the Stiperstone Hills.

Who could not be beguiled by some of Shropshire's delightful place names, such as Stiperstones, Snailbeach, Pontesbury, Crowsnest, Minsterley, Pulverbatch, Meadowtown, Cruckmeole and Squilver. The first five were connected with a wooded area some seven miles south-west of Shrewsbury. This hilly area, the Stiperstone range of hills has on its northern flanks a district once full of industry. There are ruined buildings with a tall chimney stack, timber headstocks to mine shafts, remains of adits into the hills above, with one including a date stone of 1848. There are several areas where narrow gauge railway tracks are still in-situ. Here lie the clues to what was once a thriving industry and its associated transport system.

A 6½ mile (10.4km) standard gauge branch line was built from Cruckmeole Junction on the Cambrian Railway line, south of Shrewsbury to Minsterly, jointly run by the GWR and the LNWR in 1862 primarily

This photo shows the elevated timber trestle exchange siding at Pontesbury yard with the narrow gauge line on top. The various minerals would be discharged by hopper wagon to the standard gauge wagons below. They were not very health and safety conscious at that time!

A similar view further along the timber trestle showing the standard gauge line curving away to the right of the picture.

to serve the stone quarries of the Ceiriog Great Consols Co near Habberley. Midway along the branch line was Pontesbury station, which opened on February 14, 1862 and closed to passengers in 1951 although the line continued with freight traffic until closure in 1967.

Pontesbury had a loop siding from which two sidings turned out; one was covered over by a timber trestle supporting a 2ft 4in (711mm) narrow gauge track with an opening along its length between the rails. This enabled hopper wagons to discharge directly into the larger standard gauge wagons beneath.

The Snailbeach and District

This photo of the 1920s shows the two road engine shed with locomotive No.2 *Skylark* a Class 0-4-2T built by Kerr Stuart in 1902 on the track bypassing the shed to the mine. The locomotive outside the shed is No.4, one of the USA Baldwin 4-6-0T locomotives originally built for the WD in 1917. The locomotive on the right hand spur is No.1 *Dennis* in the process of being dismantled.

This is No.2 *Skylark* a Class 0-4-2T loco at work in the quarry area in the 1920s.

narrow gauge industrial railway was opened in 1877 as a subsidiary of the Snailbeach Mining Co Ltd; which received an Act of Parliament on August 5, 1873. Its Incorporation permitted the building of around three miles (4.8km) of track from the sidings at Pontesbury to Crowsnest (Snailbeach Wharf) up on the western flank of the Stiperstone hills. There was to be an extension of about two miles (3.2km) from Crowsnest to lead mines at Pennerley, but that never materialised.

Following the uphill climb from Pontesbury exchange siding to Crowsnest,

the narrow gauge line crossed over the Shrewsbury-Bishops Castle road by an overbridge, then through open countryside passing Callow Quarry to the left. The line then continued on a 1:37 gradient to its terminus at Snailbeach Wharf where the line ended, just beyond at Crowsnest, where a reverse siding in the backward direction, with a line gradient of 1:25 for quarter of a mile (0.4km), gave access to the engine shed and the Snailbeach Lead Mine. Crowsnest was at a 52½ft (16m) higher elevation than the exchange siding at Pontesbury.

Wharf Bridge exchange sidings were parallel to the running line just below the quarry area. Some wooden wagons are shown and a hand operated crane.

Locomotive No.3 sits outside the engine shed. This is the other USA Baldwin 4-6-0T that was ex WD built in 1916.

By 1884 one of the major lead mines had closed, halving the amount of traffic and profits. Fortunately, the Eastridge granite quarry, which was about two miles (3.2km) from Pontesbury, had opened and by 1905 a short branch had been connected to the Snailbeach line – increasing traffic and profits back to a more healthy level. A record of 38,000 tons was transported.

This quarry belonged to the Ceirog Granite Company that was a major provider to the Glyn Valley Tramway whose major director was Henry Dennis, who was also the Snailbeach chairman. A short distance from the Eastridge Quarry on the right hand side further down the western flank was a smelting works for the lead ore extracted from the mines. The gradient permitted loaded wagons to run down this section by gravity with a brakesman in control leaving the steam locomotives to take the empty wagons back uphill.

Fortunes varied over the next 10 years or so with a peak during the First World War and then dropping away by 1922 to only 3,177 tons. Also, the railway was down to one locomotive, *Dennis*, that finally had to be taken out of

Some Snailbeach & District Railway wooden hopper wagons languishing in a siding overgrown with grass and weeds.

A view of the engine shed taken in 2013 which appears in reasonable condition with its two doors painted in the oxide red of the time. The two roads into the shed are still easily seen.

service for a rebuild. Railway traffic was now reliant on gravity downhill and horses for the return journey.

The locomotives and rolling stock in operation from inception to 1922 were as follows; the first steam locomotive was *Belmont* and 0-4-0 saddle tank built by Hughes Falcon Works in 1874, but acquired by the railway three years later. It was finally scrapped in 1912. The second loco was *Fernhill*, an 0-6-0

saddle tank built by Stephen Lewin in 1875, to be followed by *Dennis* built by Bagnall's, the 0-6-0 tank locomotive being named after the chairman of the Snailbeach Railway.

When this totally deplorable state of affairs arose in 1922, Colonel Stephens of light railway fame was contacted at his office in Tonbridge, Kent with a view of turning around the fortunes of this ailing railway. He and others formed a new board of directors

This is the original track that bypassed the engine shed and curved round towards the mine.

and by early 1923 set about the
unenviable task of replacing
infrastructure, locomotives and
rolling stock. An awful lot of
sleepers were rotting and were
replaced by cut-up standard gauge
ones; wagons were replaced by
some that were surplus from the
war department.

Three working second hand
locomotives were procured, but
were required to be converted
to 2ft 4in (711mm) gauge. The
first was *Skylark*, a Class 0-4-2T
No.802 built by Kerr Stuart in
1902 to 2ft 6in (762mm) gauge
for Lovatt & Co of Hartington,
Derby. After a succession of
owners it came to Snailbeach
from the War Department. This
loco became Snailbeach No.2.
Dennis was No.1 and was then
being dismantled.

The other two locomotives
were built in the USA by Baldwin
for the War Department and then
surplus to requirements. They
were 4-6-0T locomotives built to
1ft 11½in (597mm) gauge and
numbered WD 538 built in 1916
and WD 722 built in 1917. They
were numbered Snailbeach No.3
& 4 respectively.

It was reported that the
wagon fleet in 1877 totalled 53.
There were 12 timber wagons for carrying
the lead ore, all of four wheels with a capacity
of three tons. They had a chute between the
wheels which was 1ft 7in (483mm) with a
wheelbase of 4ft 7in (1397mm), length overall
of 7ft 6in (2286mm). The rest consisted
of 29 coal wagons, six timber wagons and
six goods wagons. The number of vehicles
appeared to vary, but by 1922, due to years
of use and minimal maintenance, the total
stock had fallen to eight mineral wagons and
four timber trucks. The wagons were painted
light grey with black ironwork and SDR
painted in white letters. Colonel Stephens
then purchased some surplus War Department
wagons to increase the fleet numbers.

As time went by it seemed that the

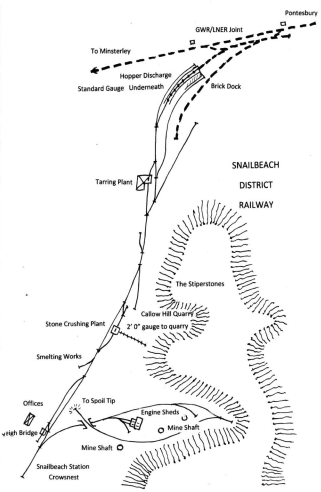

investment that Stephens had made did not
improve the railway's fortunes although there
was an increase from mine waste, gravel,
feldspar and barytes traffic that was mined near
Crowsnest. Several lead mines had closed, but
in 1928 the stone tonnage increased to 4,821
from the Callow Hill Quarry. A loop siding
was laid by the Snailbeach and a crushing plant
was built over the line where the crushed stone
was loaded directly into wagons that then went
in 3s or 4s under gravity to the loading dock at
Pontesbury.

A locomotive ran light to Pontesbury and
hauled the wagons back to the siding at Callow
hill and then ran light to the shed at Crowsnest
where it waited a day or two for the next run
to Pontesbury. This was probably not a very
efficient way to run a railway.

By 1946 the Snailbeach was once again without any locomotives as they had all failed their boiler inspections. The only solution was to hire a Fordson tractor, BUX 174, that could run with rear wheels either side of the rails and the small front ones between the rails.

On April 14, 1947, Shropshire County Council effectively became the sole owner of the railway. The locomotives were cut up in 1951 and the track from Callow Hill to Crowsnest removed. By 1962 the track was lifted down to Pontesbury with some being sold to the Talyllyn preserved railway in Wales.

One of the original point levers made by Ashbury & Co. Ltd. Manchester and dated 1881. This one is located just before the engine shed.

A part of the ruins of the old lead mine at Snailbeach, which is now preserved and of course the reason this little railway was built in the first place.

The Snibston Colliery & Swannington Railway

A photo of Glenfield station with Glenfield tunnel in the distance. Local heritage groups now have interesting walks through the tunnel when conditions allow.

Coal mining in Leicestershire goes back to the 13th century and was centred around the Swannington area in the west of the county and by the beginning of the 1800s it was the most important commodity in fuelling the industrial age.

The coal from the area was being transported by horse and cart to Leicester, which was a heavy, mucky and time-consuming job and was at a financial disadvantage compared with Nottinghamshire miners who were transporting their coal by barges on the Erewash Canal and Soar Navigation to Leicester, faster and cheaper. The answer came in 1831 with the

This is the old 1:17 incline near Swannington that was operated by a piston valve stationary engine and commenced operating in 1833 but had continuous problems for some time. It could raise three wagons of coal (18 tons) or lower six empty ones. The incline closed in 1948. In 1845 the line was extended to Burton-on-Trent and the incline was bypassed by a new line, rendering the incline as a short branch.

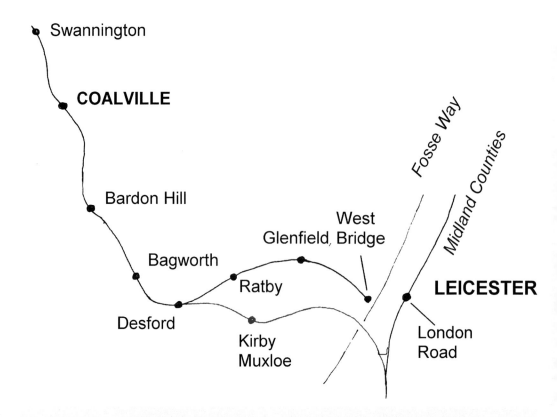

construction of a railway. John Ellis, MP and businessman, contracted George Stephenson and his son Richard to build a railway from Swannington to Leicester with the aim of delivering Leicestershire coal to Leicester at a fair price.

The line opened in stages; there was an incline at Swannington that was troublesome in the early stages and was not fully operational until 1834. It proved necessary to build Glenfield tunnel of 1,790yds (1,637m) near Groby, just outside Leicester – the longest tunnel in the world at that time. The first part of the line was opened on July 17, 1832 and the whole 16 miles (25.6km) was fully opened by end of 1833 and already delivering coal more cheaply than from the Erewash Valley.

At a later date the line was extended west to Burton upon Trent, making it accessible from both ends and reducing economic isolation. The early coal trains consisted of 24 wagons of 32 cwt each and there was a demand by the local population for passenger carrying. To oblige, a carriage was hurriedly constructed

and the line was soon carrying 60 passengers a day.

The coal trade was then expanding rapidly and the hamlet of Long Lane became the town of Coalville as houses were built to accommodate the increasing number of minors. The new railway ran through this area and in 1833 Robert Stephenson opened a colliery (No.1) at Snibston, a stone's throw from Coalville. By 1846 the Leicester and Swannington Railway had been absorbed into the Midland Railway whose chairman by that time was John Ellis.

Following the opening of colliery No.1, two more collieries were opened and operational by 1854. The three shafts (collieries) had been opened close to each other but No.3 closed in 1895 followed by No.1 with from flooding problems, leaving Snibston No.2 to continue producing. It was known affectionately by the locals as 'Snibby'.

Snibston's rail sidings, although in the care of a small group of internal plate layers, were not in best condition with a lack of track

This shows two of Snibston's colliery locomotives after closure. The nearest is a Hunslet 0-6-0DH No. 6294 built in 1965 and its companion is an English Electric 0-6-0DH built at Vulcan Foundry in 1967.

ballasting and general maintenance, mainly because of poor funding that prevented necessary improvements. However, on January 1, 1947 all collieries were nationalised and became a part of the National Coal Board (NCB) – at which time Snibston's coal output was recorded as 300,000 tons per year.

The following decades saw Snibston flourish with the Coal Board improving and making further developments on the site with a drift mine opened in the 60s with a ramp leading to the coal seam. By the 1970s the

Clean Air Act of 1956 was beginning to make itself felt, as electricity and North Sea gas were heating British homes. Gas was also being progressively taken up by industry, plus coal was no longer used for firing steam locomotives since British Railways was switching to electric and diesel locomotives.

Coal production at 'Snibby' ceased on December 16, 1983 and the railway lines were partially dismantled and abandoned. The associated buildings were taken over and managed by Leicestershire County

A view showing the sidings for coal wagons after closure with Asphalt thrown across the rails for ease of access for various demolition tasks and conversion to a coal museum. Also, the rare twin headstock of No.1 Pit Top which houses two shaft lifts can be seen on the left.

Another view of the colliery looking in the opposite direction with the twin headstock to the rear on the right. There is nothing around apart from a small trolley at the end of a siding.

Council (LCC), which built the Discovery Museum on the site. Unfortunately, LCC closed the museum in 2015 so that the site could be redeveloped.

The locomotives used on site at the point of closure were two Hunslet 0-6-0DH, Nos. 6294 & 6295 built in 1965, plus an English Electric built at Vulcan Foundry, 0-6-0DH No. 1200.

This shows the early days of the colliery museum with some old coal wagons in situ and pit head gear in the background. It all looks a little unreal.

A fine example of a Snibston Colliery coal wagon in preservation.

Glenfield Tunnel was the major engineering feature for the infant Leicester and Swannington Railway, precursor to the Midland Railway, bringing coal to Leicester from the Coalville area.

West Street Station, Leicester was the terminus for the L&SR, seen here in later LMSR days when the line was taken over by the latter company.

Southampton Docks and its Railways

The South Western Hotel was previously the Imperial Hotel built in 1872 in Canute Road that was a frequent overnight stay for passengers sailing from Southampton or for arrivals from abroad who will then take the train to London the next morning.

Southampton Docks on the Hampshire coast is almost a household name, as it must bring to mind many different episodes of large ships leaving and returning to the UK for a variety of reasons. For most of us today it means boarding large cruise ships for a luxury holiday to another part of the world and returning after a sunny and well fed, relaxing couple of weeks.

Southampton Docks is situated at the confluence of the rivers Test and Itchen, being six miles (9.6km) upstream on Southampton Water from the Solent. The Docks go back a long way and over the last 150 years have expanded and changed to meet the demands of each decade. It has seen its docks put to a wide variety of uses, often with the assistance of its

This photo shows the Pullman train arriving at the flying boat station inside the dock area. The locomotive is an H15 4-6-0 built by LSWR at Eastleigh Works in 1914 and was withdrawn from service in 1957. The terminal was in service from 1948 to 1958.

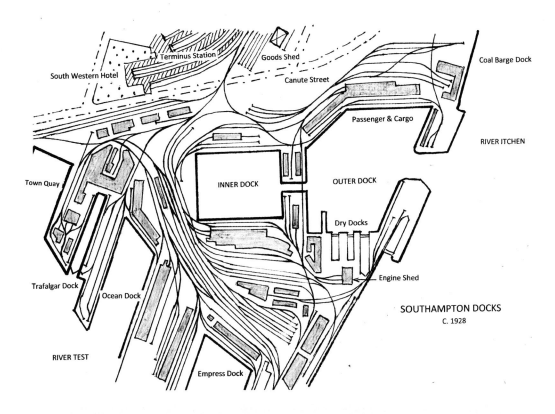

SOUTHAMPTON DOCKS
C. 1928

own complex and vast internal standard gauge railway that had access to the national network.

The earliest shipping quays were built on the northern bank of the river Itchen with a dock devoted to coal barges. Following these early quays, a large area was developed to provide four large docks, firstly the Outer Dock in 1843, the Inner Dock in 1851, Empress Dock in 1890, Ocean Dock (previously White Star Dock) in 1911 and dry docks, with additional quays following by 1902.

With an eye on profitable expansion the London and South Western Railway (LSWR) built and opened a terminus (Southampton Docks Station) in 1840 on the north side of Canute Street that separated the docks

A postcard, circa 1950, looking across the River Test at the Flying Boat Terminal with a Sunderland flying boat G-AGJN and a packed Hythe commuter ferry making across to the Southampton ferry quay.

Some of the earliest locomotives used at the docks were Alexander Shanks & Son's 0-4-0STs built in 1872, delivered in 1876 and named *Sir Bevis* and *Ascupart*. Two more followed in 1876 named *Southampton* and *Cowes*. All locomotives were fitted with condenser pipes. They were used to ferry trains from the Town station to the Royal Pier.

This early postcard shows the Royal Pier with the railway tracks and a paddle steamer tied to the jetty.

from the town and in 1882 the LSWR took over control of the whole dock complex. The station had two platforms, an engine shed with some sidings added a little later and, as time moved, on a turntable and more sidings. The port soon became a major facility for the import and export of goods throughout the British Empire together with the constant flow of passenger traffic.

Even during these early days the railway had begun to infiltrate the dock areas from a rail crossing over Canute Street with several other lines fanning out to service various quays and warehouses.

The author's model of Dugald Drummond's personal Class F9 4-4-2T locomotive with integral inspection coach named 'The Bug'. Built in 1899, it was stored at Eastleigh after his death in 1912 and finally 'killed off' in 1940.

Alongside the rail terminus was the opulent Imperial Hotel that became the South Western Hotel (of course) and was a regular overnight stay for passengers waiting for their onward travel by train or ship. By 1891 three additional platforms and an island platform had been constructed with goods and parcel traffic relocated to a new goods shed at St Lawrence Road just east of the station.

Inside the dock area a myriad of lines expanded to serve all the cargo and passenger sheds, many of which are familiar names today such as P&O (Peninsular and Oriental), Union Line (for South Africa), American Line, White Star Line and Cunard from 1919. There were berths and piers for fruit imports, local ferries and from 1919 to 1958 piers for flying boats where passengers came down from London by train (often Pullman coaches) to disembark on the pier and then join their plane. The airlines included, from the early days, Imperial Airways to BOAC towards the end.

An LSWR Class B4 0-4-0T locomotive built in 1893 by Adams and is one of 14 that worked in the dock area easily negotiating the sharp curves. They were all given names associated with destinations from the port to the Channel Islands and France. This one is *Granville* and spent most of its working life in the dock area or at Eastleigh and was withdrawn in 1963.

LB&SCR D1 Class 0-4-2T and originally known as 'D-Tanks'. A total of 125 were built between 1873 and 1887 of which some were employed to move heavier loads around the dock area.

During the 1950s and 60s some of the original sheds were replaced with what we would recognise today as multi-storey terminals to accommodate the transatlantic 'Queens'. These terminals improved the efficiency and speed of embarking/disembarking of passengers on one level and cargo on others. They were almost stations in their own right, offering all the normal expectations of a rail traveller. They had platforms, waiting rooms, baggage handling, cafes and newsagents. Special named boat-trains ran from London Waterloo to and from the Ocean Terminal with names including 'The Statesman' (SS *United States*), 'The Cunarder' (RMS *Queen Mary* and RMS *Queen Elizabeth*) and 'Union Castle Express' (Union Castle Ships to South Africa).

Refrigerated perishables would be transferred immediately to an awaiting freight train to be taken to the London markets. By the very nature of the docks' layout most sidings involved sharp curves, necessitating powerful steam locomotives with small wheelbases capable of pulling and pushing heavy wagons and coaches.

From the early 1900s onwards, the number of locomotives increased. The LSWR became a part of Southern Railway in the 1923 Big Four grouping and was then absorbed into the nationalised British Railways in 1948. Apart from boat trains from London there was an average of 20 locomotives working the docks area and a brick built engine shed with three roads opened dockside in 1847 with watering

An example of war damage inside Southampton Docks. During a German bombing raid in 1942 the warehouse of Hibbert's Ales & Lager was severely damaged and fire raged inside. There are plenty of onlookers wondering if their supply of beer will be affected.

Oliver Bulleid, the Southern's chief engineer, purchased 14 of these very beefy ex S100 Class USA 0-6-0Ts from the War Department and put them to work in Southampton Docks. They earned the name of 'Yankee Tanks'. Some have survived into preservation and the one shown is dutifully employed on the Kent and East Sussex Railway.

and coaling facilities, but by 1962 steam was being replaced by diesel locomotives.

Taking a look at the locomotives on-site over the years, the earliest was an 0-4-0 saddle tank with condenser pipes built in 1872 by Alexander Shanks and Son and named *Sir Bevis*. It was delivered four years later with companion named *Ascupart*. These locomotives were used for a transfer service between the Town station and Royal Pier for the Channel Islands, Le Havre and Isle of Wight ferries. Later, in 1876, two more were delivered and named Southampton and Cowes.

The chief engineer of the LSWR was Dugald Drummond and he was originally based at Nine Elms. During 1899, he had built his own personal inspection saloon that he used to take him to and from work back to his

This is a LB&SCR Class E2 0-6-0T locomotive that British Railways, Southern Region, decided to try out in Southampton Docks. This class dates back to around 1916, but the 16ft (4.87m) wheelbase made for difficulties negotiating the tight curves, so its use was limited.

During 1962 14 Class 07 diesel-electric shunters, built by Ruston & Hornsby were introduced into Southern Region, working mainly in Southampton Docks to replace the 'Yankee Tanks'. After admirable service they were gradually withdrawn between May 1973 and July 1977 as the work in the docks reduced.

home in Surbiton, Surrey and for inspection tours of his LSWR network. It was a class F9 4-4-2T that included an integral coach and was nicknamed 'The Bug'. He then transferred his base to Eastleigh in easy reach of Southampton Docks. Drummond died in 1912 and this composite transport was laid aside at Eastleigh until 1932 when it was refitted to conform to Southern Railway standards and used to convey important people to view the extension

to Southampton Docks. Sadly, 'The Bug' was killed off in 1940 after just 41 years.

Another early arrival into the docks was the LSWR 0-4-0T Class B4 that was originally designed for station piloting and dock shunting especially where sharp curves were normal. It was ideal for the Southampton Dock network. A total of 25 B4s were built by the LSWR at Nine Elms between 1891 and 1893 and by 1900 around 14 were used

A car transporter around 2016 unloading BMW Minis from Cowley, Oxford plant in Southampton dockyard ready for loading onto Ro-Ro ferries to be sold abroad.

A Red Funnel Ro-Ro ferry, Red Falcon has just left Town Quay in Southampton Docks for its short voyage to East Cowes on the Isle of Wight. Leaving Town Quay it joins the River Test and then into Southampton Water and out into the Solent to East Cowes for the 50 minute crossing.

in Southampton Docks network. These locomotives were all given names in line with the destinations of the ships sailing to the Channel Islands and France e.g., Jersey, Alderney, Trouville, Normandy, St Malo, Granville, Guernsey, Dinard etc.

Also, occasionally used was a London, Brighton & South Coast Railway (LB&SCR) 0-4-2T Class D1 locomotive known as a 'D Tank' built at Brighton works between 1873 and 1887. This type could undertake the task of shunting heavier loads and 125 were built.

The beginning of the Second World War in 1939 interfered with the normal day-to-day routines of the Docks. They were subject to heavy night bombing and devastation by the German Luftwaffe, but life carried on. In early 1944, prior to the D-Day landings in Normandy, the areas around the south coast of England became a military zone.

Two large concrete caissons were constructed in the George V dry dock then floated out to the Normandy coast to become a part of the Mulberry Harbour and at Southern Railway's Eastleigh Works, just outside Southampton they made landing craft and a host of other war material for the landings on June 6.

After the war, Britain's railways and rolling stock was in poor condition and the resident B4 and D1 locomotives in Southampton Docks were no exception, having managed

An ultra-modern cruise ship, the *Royal Princess*, at its berth in Southampton. It is the largest ship of Princess Cruises, built in Italy, and has been in operation since 2013. It can accommodate 3,560 passengers.

One of the container transport companies using the Western Docks Container Terminal is Maritime Ltd., which currently has two Class 66 EMD locomotives in its blue livery named *Maritime Intermodel One* and *Two*. This one is *Maritime Intermodel Two* No.66047. The locomotives are hired under contract with DB Cargo (UK) to allow Maritime to expand their rail intermodal haulage services to and from Southampton and Felixstowe. Hornby has released an 00 gauge model of this locomotive.

This photo is worthy of a quality brochure and does illustrate the size of the Western Docks Container Terminal. The container vessel is *Mol Triumph*, built in South Korea by Samsung Heavy Industries and is the world's largest ship at over 400m (437yds) in length. One of Maritime's articulated container trucks sits, fully loaded with containers, on the quayside. The giant container gantries relentlessly remove the containers from the ship and move along its length on their dedicated rail tracks.

the best part of 50 years' service. Southern Railway's chief mechanical engineer, Oliver Bulleid, then decided to purchase 14 ex USA 0-6-0T S100 class locomotives that were a part of 382 held in the UK by the War Department in 1943. Most of these eventually went for shipment to France after D-Day. They entered service in 1948, had a short wheelbase to cope with tight curves, were powerful and proved themselves to be effective. They earned the nickname of 'Yankee Tanks'.

During the 1950s, Southern Region, now a part of British Railways, decided to try out some ex 1916 London, Brighton & South Coast Railway (LB&SCR) 0-6-0T E2 class locomotives for some shunting duties, but with a 16ft (4.87m) wheelbase they were limited to routes where they could safely negotiate the rail curvatures in the docks.

By 1962 the decision was made to retire the 'Yankee Tanks' from shunting duties in the docks; some were redeployed on other duties in

A view of the new Freightliner container terminal at Redbridge, Southampton, which is on the west side of the dock area. The terminal will allow for loading of longer trains with up to fourteen more containers per train amounting to tens of thousands more containers being transported every year.

Queen Mary the grand Atlantic liner of the P&O Line lays beside an early Ocean Terminal building, with a Bulleid pacific of the Southern Railway on a Pullman Boat Train.

the region and five survived to the end of steam in the Southern Region. The replacement locomotives were 14 British Rail 0-6-0 Class 07 diesel-electric shunters specially built by Ruston & Hornsby and started work in 1962, providing good service until a gradual withdrawal from May 1973 to July 1977 as the docks traffic declined.

By the mid-1960s passenger numbers to Southampton Terminus (Southampton Docks Station) had sadly declined and when the Waterloo to Bournemouth main line via Southampton Central was upgraded to third rail 750V DC, it was not extended down the branch from the Northam triangle to Southampton Terminus, thus

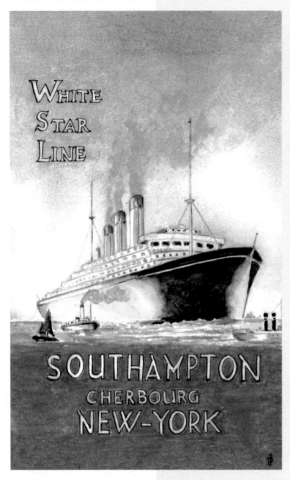

causing its inevitable closure on September 5, 1966. However, the non-electrified access line into Southampton Docks remained in use.

Today, the original dock area known as Eastern Docks has been transformed for the 21st century. The Outer Dock has been redeveloped and so-called Ocean Village Marina plus the Inner Dock has been drained, in-filled and used to park hundreds of cars prior to export from the RO-RO (Roll On-Roll Off) Terminal on the River Itchen side of the docks. They are delivered by car trains from Jaguar, Halewood and Castle Bromwich using IPA cartics and from the BMW Mini plant at Cowley, Oxford using WIA drive-through flat wagons with hoods. The Cruise Terminal, as the name implies, is for the cruise ships leaving with their holiday makers for exotic cruises around the world.

Between Eastern Docks and Western Docks is Town Quay where the Red Funnel Line, RoRo ferries, make the frequent journeys down Southampton Water across to East Cowes on the Isle of Wight. Also, small local ferry boats leave from Town Quay and ply back and forth over the River Test to Hythe Pier on the west bank where foot passengers disembark and board the small electric 2ft (610mm) narrow gauge

White Star Line poster of the 1930s with no hint of its tragedy in the loss of its newest ocean liner, the *Titanic*, outbound from Southampton.

Ocean Terminal at Southampton Docks, of the second generation after the last war. A Lord Nelson Class 4-6-0 is on the Boat Train while a diminutive 0-4-0 tank loco shunts vans.

Southampton's early Town Quay which was served by the LSWR from its Terminus via roadside track to the docks. The 0-4-0 loco was unique with condensing apparatus.

The predecessor to the Southern Railway was the LSWR where at Eastleigh Works a 4-6-0 'Paddle Box' and a Class C14 0-4-0 tank engine shunts a colourful LSWR coach.

railway, which is the oldest pier railway in the world.

Just past Town Quay is Western Docks built on reclaimed land with riverside quays for two cruise terminals, a fruit terminal and a bulk terminal. A freight spur leaves the mainline at Millbrook at the western end of Western Docks and curves around and runs east alongside the four terminals with loop sidings. Continuing west the Southampton Container Terminal continues to expand. Containers are lined up along the quayside and the freight yard is located next to the main line with loop sidings and mechanised rail container gantry cranes for loading onto the flat bed wagons. Access to the main line is from either end of the yard. A little further to the west is the new Redbridge Freightliner Terminal.

Southwold station, circa 1900, with holiday makers and their cases standing patiently on the platform waiting to catch the train to Halesworth. The unknown locomotive is just getting up steam outside the engine shed to the left of the picture.

Southwold is a charming and vibrant small town on the coast of Suffolk at the estuary of the River Blyth and faces the North Sea. Today visitors enjoy the beaches, the working lighthouse, local nature reserves and of course it is home to the well-known brewers Adnams. Because of its location there is only one main road in and out of the town, whereas for 50 years between 1879 and 1929 there was also a 3ft (914mm) narrow gauge railway. It operated between Southwold and the inland market town of Halesworth, a distance of 8.8 miles (14.1km).

Back in the early 1800s trading and fishing at the harbour was declining and affecting the wealth of the town, so the local council decided to promote Southwold as a holiday resort with an emphasis on the beaches that would be ideal for private bathing with bathing machines, good inns and lodging houses. During this period the East Suffolk Railway (ESR) was being constructed from Ipswich

One of the first locomotives on the railway was this Sharp Stewart 2-4-0T, No.1 named *Southwold* and built in 1879. It is seen here beautifully turned out in green livery for the photograph. Unfortunately, it was repossessed by Sharp Stewart in 1883.

to Yarmouth (now Great Yarmouth) and it was wrongly assumed the line would pass through or very near Southwold. Unfortunately for the town, the line swung inland to Halesworth to avoid unnecessary increases in costs to overcome geological difficulties.

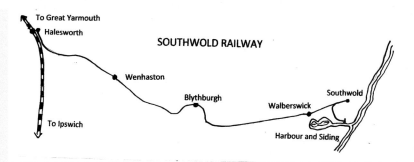

In 1855 a request was made for the ESR to build a branch line from Halesworth to Southwold but came to nothing, as did various other schemes over the following 20 years. By 1862 the ESR had been absorbed into the Great Eastern Railway (GER). In 1875, after many false hopes, it was agreed that a new 3ft (914mm) gauge railway could be constructed. The Southwold Railway Company was formed and on July 24, 1876 an Act of Parliament gave permission to begin construction. Locomotive speed was limited and a simple signalling system had to be put in place.

After the work was completed, inspected and passed by the Board of Trade on September 19, 1879 a celebration lunch took place in the Swan Hotel on September 23 with the official opening on September 24. Unfortunately, heavy rain caused flooding on the line near Wenhaston Mill but the first train completed the round trip without incident.

Within the first month of working, the company applied for a Light Railway Order, which was granted on March 11, 1880. This limited the operation to one engine in steam and a maximum speed of 16mph (25.8kph).

The construction of the railway cost £90,000 and more money was always needed as income from passenger and goods services never produced enough surplus to pay off debts. During the first 10 years, passenger traffic remained around 76,000 journeys per year, but the goods traffic doubled to 9,000 tons with steady increases in both over the following decade. Most trains were a mixture of passenger and goods wagons.

Leaving Southwold there were stations

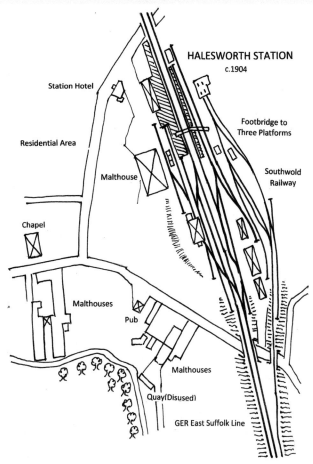

A train about to
leave Southwold
station in 1924.
The train consists
of two coaches and
two wagons with
a Sharp Stewart
2-4-0T locomotive
heading out back
end first. Note
the centre buffer
stop and coupling
and the wagon on
the right that is
probably a Moy's
coal wagon.

Train leaving
Blythburgh station
heading towards
Southwold. Trains
were often made
up for mixed
traffic, which
can be seen here
with a covered
wagon between
the locomotive
and carriage,
which was a six-
wheeler with
entrances from
open platforms
at each end. The
locomotive is
thought to be a
later replacement
from Sharp
Stewart, a 2-4-2T
engine that was
renamed No.1
Southwold.

at Walberswick, Blythburgh
and Wenhaston and finally
Halesworth where there was
interchange via a footbridge
with the East Suffolk Railway,
as the Southwold Railway had
its own passenger and goods
terminus adjacent to the main
line. The signals were semaphore
type with a signal arm on either
side of the post to accommodate
trains from each direction and
were interlocked with the points
at each station and operated by
ground leavers. Being single line,
operational safety was assured
by the use of the Train Staff and
Ticket system. Apart from the
main line, each station had its
own sidings for mixed goods and
coal and a loop line at Blythburgh
and Wenhaston stations.

On the edge of Southwold
the line crossed the River Blyth

using a small viaduct with a swing bridge in the centre. To ensure that no accidents occurred, the bridge centre span was secured by an Annett's Key, which was attached to the Train Staff. As the name suggests, the span had a lock that could only be opened by the special key allowing the bridge to be swung open and closed by hand. These have been widely used in the past for securing point leavers and ground frames. By 1907 the wooden bridge piling was inadequate and a replacement bridge was built using steel piling and angular steel girders. Apart from the swing bridge over the River Blyth, there were 13 small bridges over the length of the line. At this time the River Blyth was still navigable to Halesworth.

By 1914 a short branch had been built to Harbour Quay with a view of revitalising the fishing industry and general trade, but

A mixed train approaching Wenhaston station hauled by unknown 2-4-0T locomotive. Note the single post bi-directional semaphore signal with the red and green night lenses and oil lamp in the middle. The night lenses are probably positioned lower down the post to enable easier filling of the lamp. The signal is operated by basic rodding back to Wenhaston station.

A six-wheeled coal wagon of Thomas Moy, the local coal merchants. Each wagon had three compartments with drop-down gates on both sides.

A nicely posed photo of the early 1900s at Southwold of the staff, engine driver and fireman together with a number of fish transport baskets, cases and a trunk. The locomotive is probably a 2-4-0T with two coaches behind.

A view of Halesworth GER station on extreme left with the terminus of the Southwold Railway to the right. There is a covered shed over the siding and a wharf for transfer of goods to the standard gauge sidings in the centre.

The last locomotive to be procured was in 1914 to take on the extra heavier load resulting from the First World War activity at the harbour. This was a Manning Wardle 0-6-2T and numbered as 4 and named *Wenhaston*. As this extra work reduced so the locomotive was used for regular work.

A view of Halesworth station looking in the Lowestoft direction with an Ipswich train about to enter the platform. This photo was probably taken in the 1940s, well after the closure of the Southwold Railway, but the transfer sidings, wharf and goods shed are still standing and the standard gauge wagons are still using the two sidings.

Halesworth station today serves Greater Anglia trains and still has most of the original buildings on the town side. It is also the home of the Halesworth Museum, while the opposite platform just has a small shelter and a seat. To the right of that platform is greensward and trees that was once occupied by the transfer sidings and terminus of the Southwold Railway.

the First World War saw hopes of that dashed. The branch was useful for some war work to transfer coal and goods to the small fleet of naval ships anchored in the estuary. In 1923 the railway became a part of the London North Eastern Railway (LNER).

Closure

The little railway jogged along after the war, but as the road network improved and motor buses and lorries started to increase the railway lost business. It tried reducing fares to encourage passengers, but its income continued to fall and was soon losing money. This was also a bad time economically as by 1930 the general depression had set in. It was soon evident that financial support would not be forthcoming and the railway was forced to close on April 11, 1929. The last train to leave Southwold left at 5.25pm and returned at 7.20pm. Needless to say the train with its four carriages was packed with people to wish the railway farewell. Crowds lined the route waving their sad goodbyes.

The once delightful narrow gauge Southwold Railway in Suffolk, with a locomotive and white coach depicting the last of several livery changes that the company made. On the left is an engine shed for one of the two locomotives of the railway.

Rolling stock

The passenger stock consisted of six six-wheeled carriages, some with side doors and others with end doors and outside platforms. They were quite basic with wooden seats covered in a bit of carpeting and lit by oil lamps. The outsides were originally painted white with black lettering and later painted a dull red with white lettering. There was no continuous or vacuum braking system, just a hand brake and one buffer was situated centrally at each end with loose couplings.

Goods wagons

During the 50 years of operating, the wagon count had increased to 39 consisting of mainly four- and six-wheeled open trucks; the latter being used to transport coal for Thomas Moy Ltd., plus two four-wheeled closed wagons with sliding doors used mainly for passenger luggage.

Locomotives

The railway started life with three Sharp Stewart 2-4-0T steam locomotives built in 1879 numbered 1, 2 and 3 and named *Southwold*, *Halesworth* and *Blyth* respectively and were painted dark green. By 1881 the railway was struggling to repay its debts and Loco No.1 was repossessed by Sharp Stewart. By 1893, with an increase in passenger numbers and goods, the railway was forced to buy another locomotive from Sharp Stewart, a slightly longer 2-4-2T and was renamed No.1 *Southwold*. In 1914 a Manning Wardle 0-6-2T number 4 named *Wenhaston* was procured to take on the extra work resulting from the war effort on the Harbour branch. It was later used to haul regular trains. Loco No.1 was scrapped in 1929 and 2, 3, and 4 in 1941. At some stage locos 1, 2, and 3 were painted G.E.R. blue and before closure were painted black, leaving No.4 in dark green.

Today, the Southwold Railway Trust is committed to restoring this little railway and recreating the atmosphere of those times.

Surrey Border & Camberley Railway

A train headed up by an unknown 4-6-2 leaves Camberley station for Farnborough Green. The double span roof can be clearly seen with the signal box at the extreme right of the photo and the side of the turntable in the bottom right. It certainly looks popular in the days before the Second World War.

An elaborate small gauge system on the scale of the Romney Hythe and Dymchurch Railway, sadly the Surrey Border & Camberley Railway (SBCR) never had a chance to get established because of its over capitalisation and the outbreak of the second World War in 1939. The line was founded in 1938 and financed by Alexander Kinlock. It was built to the unusual gauge of 10¼in (260mm) with a track length of two miles (3.2km) connecting Farnborough Green to Camberley.

The SBCR obviously wanted to be taken seriously as Camberley station comprised five platforms with a 60ft (18.29m) x 40ft (12.19m) double span overall roof, electric lighting, public announcement system and train indicator boards. Tracks

This is a personal photo of Ian Peaty (co-author) who had a day out with his family to experience his boyhood passion for railways and is the blond lad on the left. His father is at the front, brother to Ian's right, sister behind and mother at the rear. The train is seen here passing through Cove Wood. The photograph was probably taken in 1938.

A photo taken around 1939 at Camberley with a train of happy people intending to enjoy the two-mile (3.2km) trip to Farnborough Green. An unknown 4-6-2 locomotive is at the front just about to pull away with its train of small open passenger carriages. Even the car park was full with vehicles of the era and plenty of onlookers to add to the atmosphere. Little did they know that we would be at war within months and the railway closed down and bankrupt!

in and out of the station were controlled by a signal gantry with a signal box overlooking the entire station, which included coach sidings and locomotive depot. The railway was open all year round so that it could be relied upon by commuters.

There were two intermediate stations between Farnborough Green and Camberley being Cove Wood and Watchetts Wood, all being electrically lit with the line being used by commuters as well as day trippers.

With regard to rolling stock, seven Pacific type steam locomotives designed by C. S.

Bullock, an aircraft engineer working at nearby Farnborough, were built between 1931 and 1937. Five of these superb locos were supplied to the SBCR with one 2-6-0+0-6-2 Garratt loco built by Kitson of Leeds in 1938. Livery was green with red coach lining and passengers were accommodated in open sided bogie coaches. There were also some Pullman style coaches and a couple of slip coaches that were used on occasions.

Like all new ventures, marketing your product to the public is always important and as this was a new railway a

A posed photograph of locomotives and their drivers seen here at Farnborough Green. The locomotives are most likely to be all 4-6-2's with their open bogie carriages and some Pullman styled coaches. Farnborough Green station did not have the luxury trappings of Camberley station.

One of the ex-Surrey Border & Camberley (SB&CR) locomotives, a 10¼ (260mm) gauge 4-6-2 named *Edward VIII* seen here at Eastleigh. It was built in 1936 by H Bullock, ran for a short while at Fox Hill Railway and then transferred to the SBCR in 1938 until line closure at the end of 1939 because of the war. Fortunately it saw service on other railways after the war and went to Eastleigh Lakeside Railway in 2007.

substantial amount of money had already been spent on the infrastructure and rolling stock, leaving the railway short of cash and it had run into serious financial debt by late 1939. In September 1939 the UK found itself thrust into the Second World War and the railway closed for the duration. It was declared bankrupt in the November of that year and the railway never reopened. It was, no doubt, a sad loss as it was out to prove that it was a superb narrow gauge railway.

Fortunately two of these magnificent Pacific locos have been saved and restored, giving excellent service at the Eastleigh Lakeside Railway at the Country Park, south of Eastleigh in Hampshire, which was opened in 1992. This railway continues an unusual theme of twin gauges, the 10¼in gauge for the old SBCR locos and 7¼in gauge for the Eastleigh locomotives.

This is *Silver Jubilee* proudly displayed at the Eastleigh Lakeside Railway in Hampshire. It is a 10¼ins (260mm) gauge, 4-6-2 locomotive No. 2005 and was built in 1935 by Herbert Bullock during King George V's Silver Jubilee year. It ran on three small railway ventures before entering service on the Surrey Border & Camberley Railway in 1938, which was, of course, short lived.

T.W. Ward, Scrap Merchants of Grays, Essex

This was taken in September 1982 at the Thomas W. Ward, Columbia Wharf scrapyard at Grays in Essex. The locomotive is *Hengist*, a Robert Stephenson & Hawthorn 0-4-0 262hp diesel built in 1962, No. 8367 to Bagnall design. It was previously employed at the CEGB Richborough power station in Kent.

This once world-renowned business situated on the side of the River Thames in Grays, Essex was founded by Thomas W. Ward in 1878 as a coal and coke merchants. The business was in close contact with both collieries and several railway companies, a situation which no doubt inspired this progressive company to seek other avenues of business as it soon moved into dealing with

A view from the River Thames end of Ward's pier in 1983 with a ship on the left being broken down into its scrap parts. The locomotive is *Hengist* and the two rail cranes will load up the wagons behind.

This is a Barclay 0-4-0 diesel locomotive of unknown works number in 1985, probably built around 1970, sitting idle at the beginning of a jetty. Note a fixed crane to the left and a rail crane to the right of the loco.

scrap metal, including machinery.

By the 1920s, Ward's was claiming to be the "premier ship-breaking firm in the world". Ship-breaking yards were not only at Grays, but also at Preston, Barrow in Furness, Morecombe, Pembroke Dock, Milford Haven and Lelant. At Milford Haven, Ward's formed a subsidiary company, The Milford Haven Dock and Railway Company.

In 1934, the W. S. Laycock Company of Sheffield was acquired, which increased the presence of Ward's into the railway business, as Laycock's built railway carriages, locomotive underframes and also parts for the automotive industry. New areas of business included the provision of railway sidings to new factories

and equipping them with plant and machinery, no doubt thanks to Ward's earlier connections with Sheffield. New business included the supply and erection of steel-framed buildings, bridges and building works at collieries. Ward's had formed specialist departments for engineers and railways who built and laid sidings and points to the expanding firms. By the mid-1950s, Ward's employed 11,500 people.

Demolition of buildings, especially those with metal framework, was a major part of the 'scrap' business, and Ward's highlight in this area must have been the demolition of London's Crystal Palace.

Ward's diversified into several areas

Hengist on the move with specially adapted large steel scrap wagons to contain the vast amounts of scrap picked up by the claws of the rail crane and caterpillar crane.

A BR 0-6-0 Class 08 diesel shunter at the BR exchange sidings at Grays with the spur to Thomas Ward to the right. The diesel is seen here pushing the bogie bolster wagons of steel girders towards an adjacent dock area next to Thomas Wards, which are for the redevelopment of that area.

This photo of 1985 is not one of activity, but of a site nearing closure. A lone Barclay 0-4-0 diesel and an empty 15 ton steel wagon stand on the jetty while an electric rail crane with grab and a fixed crane are idle. To the right on the Kent side of the River Thames is one of the two giant pylons that carry the heavy duty power cables between Essex and Kent. A small tanker sails up stream to its destination.

of allied businesses such as a brickworks and stone quarries. In 1928, the Ketton Portland Cement Works was founded on 1,170 acres in the county of Rutland with its private railway system laid by the firm. This company had become a core activity of Ward's by the late 1970s. Their De Lank Granite Quarry in Cornwall supplied top quality granite for London's Tower Bridge and also the Blackfriars railway bridge.

The quarry was connected by a one and a half mile (2.4km) standard gauge mineral line to the Wenford Bridge terminus of the Wenford Bridge branch of the Bodmin and Wadebridge Railway. This branch was six and a half miles (10.4km) long from Wenford Bridge to the junction at Dunmere. In 1981, the company divided into three divisions; raw materials (scrap metal), industrial supplies and industrial dismantling. A

The two steel wagons are being loaded up with scrap by the rail crane with the claw and from the caterpillar crane with its claw. The driver takes a break.

year later, RTZ (Rio Tinto Zinc) a British/ Australian multinational metals and mining corporation, acquired a major shareholding and a takeover was made in early 1982. Thomas W. Ward (Roadstone) was sold to Ready Mixed Concrete in 1988.

The ship-breaking business at Grays in Essex, on the north bank of the River Thames, was squeezed between the Grays Portland Cement Works upstream and downstream a timber yard and railway sleepers depot with a wharf and jetty, both served by sidings from the London, Tilbury and Southend Railway. The Grays Cement Works, formerly Brooks Works and Anchor Works, was just one of the several similar firms. This one was founded in 1871 and later became a part of the large Associated Portland Cement Manufactures (APCM) conglomerate in 1900, the site closing down in 1922.

After both world wars, there were many warships that the Royal Navy no longer required. Among these were the massive Dreadnought-type battleships, which ended

Another photo of *Hengist* standing idle on the jetty. This view is looking down stream and as the River Thames bends around to the right the cranes of Tilbury Docks can be seen. When the Thomas Ward site closed *Hengist* was transferred to T J Thompson &Son Ltd, scrap merchants in Stockton.

Although work at a scrapyard would not be everyone's choice, this is a rather sad scene at the end of an era with a few bits of scrap iron and the electric rail crane with its electro- magnetic sat on the ground. This view is looking from the River Thames and shows the rail link curving to the right down to the BR on the London, Tilbury and Southend Railway.

their days at Ward's Columbia Wharf for breaking up; there were 19 in all from the First World War broken up at Grays. Since those days, many smaller coastal ships have made their last journeys to this scrapyard. With the onset of closure of the Inner London Docks during the 1960s, the traditional lighterage by tugs and barges loading and unloading in mid-stream diminished. Over 40 barges and tugs were scrapped and Ward's Columbia Wharf dealt with much of this business.

The jetty had two railway sidings and two rail mounted cranes that continuously loaded the scrap metal into rail wagons for onward transport to steel works or alternatively, loaded onto coastal ships for export. The scrapyard railway system was connected via exchange sidings to the London Tilbury & Southend Railway (LT&SR) with a single rail siding into the timber yard and rail sleeper depot. Shunting was carried out by a British Rail 08 class diesel locomotive.

Ward's private rail system at Columbia Wharf in the 1980s had two resident diesel shunting locomotives. *Hengist* was a Robert Stephenson & Hawthorne diesel hydraulic 0-4-0, No 8367, built in 1962 to Bagnall

design, which had previously worked at the CEGB Richborough Power Station in Kent located by the River Stour and was resplendent in bright yellow with red wheels and motion. The other 0-4-0 diesel loco was built by F. C. Hibberd of Park Royal, to works No 3641 built in 1953.

Many another loco worked its last days at the Columbia Wharf, Grays; some were resold while most built during the 1950s were cut-up. In the period of 1976 there were four diesels to be seen, including two built by John Fowler, and one each by Hibberd's and Ruston & Hornsby. Heavy duty steel wagons were used for internal purposes with standard wagons being filled with small broken up scrap metal for onward delivery to steel mills. Two rail-mounted cranes with magnets dealt with the ferrous metals, while the more valued copper and brass was taken out of the ships and dealt with separately.

In 1982 the company was split into three and sold off to RTZ, Henry Boot and Readymix Concrete.

Tilbury Docks and its Railway

A view of Fenchurch Street station in 2010. It was originally built in 1851 for the London and Blackwall Railway, but was rebuilt in 1854 when agreement was reached with the London, Tilbury & Southend Railway (LT&SR) for both companies to use the station. It is small by London Termini standards as it has only four platforms and they are kept very busy. It serves East London and Essex down to Southend and Shoeburyness.

London's docks were once the symbol of Britain's industrial might and the development of its Empire. The docks were built in 1799 to 1815 downstream from the City to the Wapping area on the north bank of the River Thames. This was known as the Pool of London, with numerous warehouses for the importation of spices, coffee, tea, ivory, meat and vegetables from the British Empire. With an increasing population and trade with sailing ships

The workhorses of the LT&SR were the 4-4-2T locomotives, which included the similar classes 37, 51 and 79, built between 1909 and 1930 by several manufacturers over that time. Only one has survived into preservation, No. 80 *Thundersley*, Class 79 built by Robert Stephenson & Co. in 1909 and withdrawn in the early 1950s. It is a part of the National Collection and on display at Bressingham Steam Park, Norfolk.

A view over
Tilbury Docks
yard and shed in
1959.

giving way to steam power, there was little room for expansion and development. Ships were becoming increasingly larger and requiring greater depths for berths and so a new docking area became necessary downstream. The London docks were badly damaged by bombing during the Second World War and continual strikes and labour unrest in the 1950s and 60s hastened their demise. Final closure came in 1969.

Tilbury Docks in Essex opened in a small way as early as 1886. In 1909, as passenger and freight traffic increased, Tilbury became a part of the Port of London Authority (PLA) which encouraged several major schemes of development with a new Cruise Terminal built

in 1930 which incorporated the Riverside Station.

As passenger and freight business continues to change, the port has to adapt its handling of cargo and to constantly monitor the changing needs of passengers. At Tilbury Port the P&O line has used its services since 1903 and with the new London Cruise Terminal larger ships such as the *Arcadia* and *Iberia* can berth, together with the older *Black Watch* ship taking passengers to the Baltic Sea ports and Scandinavia.

The Port of London Authority (PLA) extended the dock areas during the 1960s with a larger, modern dock one mile (1.6km) from the main dock and built a large grain terminal

Tilbury Docks
shed during 1961
with a standard
9F 2-10-0, No.
92201, built at BR
Swindon Works
in 1959 for mainly
freight haulage in
Eastern Region.
It was withdrawn
from service on
July 31, 1966. It
certainly looks
uncared for in this
photo.

This diagram shows the layout of the new Construction Material Aggregate Terminal (CMAT) and Ro-Ro ferry area together with the red lines that indicate the spurs to both rail heads. This large scale development is on the old Tilbury Power station site.

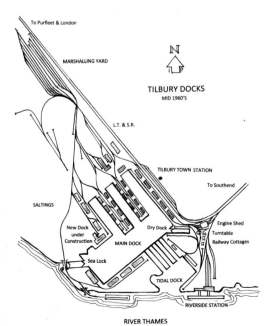

with silos, plus a new container terminal. During this time Tilbury played its part in saying 'goodbye' to the many who emigrated to Australia under the '£10 Poms' scheme and where immigrants from the Colonies, especially the West Indies, arrived to be greeted by our cold climate.

Tilbury Port was privatised in 1992 and the old Riverside rail station that witnessed all the comings and goings finally closed its doors and was renovated as the luggage retrieval hall for the new London Cruise

Tilbury Riverside station with its platforms and train stabling sidings during the 1970s after the LTSR had been electrified to 25kV AC catenary system in 1961. The trains were Class 302 EMUs that commenced service on the LT&SR in 1962 and were built at the BR York Works and Doncaster. There were 112 of four-car, slam door sets, had a maximum speed of 75mph (120kph), were refurbished between 1981 and 1982 and finally withdrawn in 1999 after 37 years' service.

A Class 302 No. 302240 at Tilbury Riverside waiting for its return journey to Fenchurch Street station during January 1984. By this time steamship services were reducing although the ferry service run by Sealink, the BR Shipping Division, between Gravesend and Tilbury was still running to a timetable. By this time future plans were being drawn up to redevelop the area into the London Cruise Terminal and the station was finally closed in 1992.

Terminal that opened in 1995. Tilbury Port has its competitors in the UK for container traffic, especially with Felixstowe and the latest operator London Gateway, but cruising from Tilbury continues grow.

In its heyday the port had an established rail network dealing with large volumes of freight and passengers with immediate connection to the London, Tilbury and Southend Railway (LT&SR) that ran along the north bank of the Thames from Fenchurch Street Terminal in the City of London to Southend Central and Shoeburyness. From Fenchurch Street the line then split into two large loops at Barking with the lower line accessing the more industrial Thameside areas including Rainham, Purfleet, Grays, Tilbury Town, Stanford-le-Hope and joining the upper loop at Pitsea. The upper loop ran through less industrial areas of Upminster, and Basildon.

To house the numerous steam locomotives used in the dock area, there were twin engine sheds with through tracks situated in the triangular

Today, c2c is the train operating company on the LT&S line and since March 2003 has been successfully operating Adtranz /Bombardier 357/2 Electrostar EMU, four-car sets. These are being phased out at the end on 2022 to be replaced by new Bombardier Aventra EMUs.

rail junction east of the Town Station, where the line continues eastward to Southend with the spur then peeling off south to the Riverside Station. There were three groups of rail workers' cottages within the triangle and for the dock workers there was the very welcome Basin Tavern pub. In 1935 there were 16 locos stationed at Tilbury and by 1960 this had increased to 20.

A variety of steam locomotives were to be seen, including Classes 4P and 4MT 2-6-4t, Class 2F 0-6-0, Class P 0-4-4t, Class 9F 2-10-0 and in 1962 an 8F 2-8-0. This latter loco was an ex-WD machine able to deal with a high volume of freight. The very popular 2-6-4t locomotives of the LT&SR were on home ground and fortunately 41966 *Thundersley* has been preserved at the Bressingham Steam Gardens in Norfolk as part of the National Railway Museum (NRM) collection.

Back to today and the LT&SR is now electrified using the 25 KV AC catenary system and modern Class 357 EMUs operated by c2c for the 39 mile (62.4km) commuter trip to London. These units are being replaced by Class 720 Aventra trains of 10 cars giving 20% more seating.

A new venture that is well underway on the old Tilbury Power Station site, and a little downstream from the old Riverside Station,

The new replacement trains for c2c will be EMU Class 720 Aventra 10-car sets giving 20% more seats. They are manufactured by Bombardier at its Derby Litchurch Lane Works and power will be standard 25kV 50Hz pantograph from overhead line.

Right: This shows the Tilbury Container Terminal with a train of containers headed up by a Class 66 No. 66431 entering the area. The locomotive entered service with Direct Rail Services (DRS) in November 2008.

is the development of a Construction Material Aggregate Terminal (CMAT) in conjunction with the major aggregates group Tarmac. This will include manufacturing, processing and a supporting railhead.

A new rail link is now completed and operational with connections from the main LT&SR main line to railheads at the Tilbury 2 CMAT facility and new Roll On, Roll Off ferry terminal which is reported to be the largest in Europe and operated by P&O Ferries. It is

Below: A train of containers entering Tilbury Container Terminal with a DRS Class 66 No. 66421 at the front that entered service with DRS in September 2007. This posed atmospheric photo was taken at night showing the train passing the silo of the Tilbury Grain Terminal.

The London, Tilbury & Southend Railway had its own individual 4-4-2 tank engines which dealt with the heavy commuter trains into London, the company being taken over by the Midland Railway who retained these smart locomotives.

expected to carry food and drink products, steel, bulk containers and automotive parts and supplies. The railways will handle a great deal of the extra traffic with loaded trains expected to be the heaviest in the UK. Three rail operating companies are expected to be involved, such as DB Cargo, Freightliner and Eddie Stobart with Direct Rail Services. Expectations of the total additional volumes created from the Tilbury 2 capacity are in the region of 16 million tonnes per annum.

Index

Acknowledgements

Background Page
11 Centre *Adrian Booth*
13 Bottom *Mark Wyard*
A Town of Brewery Railways
14 Bottom *BR*
15 Top *R C Riley*
15 Bottom *R C Riley*
16 Bottom *R C Riley*
17 Top *R C Riley*
17 Bottom *R C Riley*
18 Top *H E Lee*
Bodmin and Wadebridge
19 Top *L & G R P*
19 Bottom *L & G R P*
22 Top *L & G R P*
21 Bottom *Unknown*
20 Top *BR*
Bowaters & Sittingbourne etc
26 Both *A G Wells (SKLR Archive)*
27 Both *A G Wells (SKLR Archive)*
28 Top *A G Wells (SKLR Archive)*
28 Bottom *Tony Storey*
30 Bottom *Mjroots–Wikipedia Commons*
Dove Holes & Tunstead
37 Top *Hayden Gill – Cemex*
40 Top *Tarmac*
42 Bottom *Tarmac*
43 Both *Tarmac*
Gloucester and Warwick
44 Top *P J Garland*
Hawhurst Branch
49 Top *Wikipedia Commons*
49 Bottom *Goudhurst Local History Society (GLHS)*
50 Top *Gregory (PO 1913)*
50 Bottom *GLHS*
51 Top David Clark *(Kezlan Images)*.
   Bottom *R F Roberts*
52 Top *Wikipedia Commons*
54 Bottom *GLHS*
55 Top *S C Nash*
Mid Hants Railway
59 Bottom *Peter Lambert*
60 Bottom *Unknown*
61 Both *Andrew Fewster*
62 Both *Andrew Fewster*
63 Both *Andrew Fewster*

Morwellham Quay
65 Bottom *C Bartlett – Wikipedia Commons*
66 Top *J H Trounson Collection*
67 Top *J H Trounson Collection*
69 Top *Crispin Purdye – Wikimedia Commons*
Norfolk Railways
72 Bottom *Ben Brooksbank – Wikipedia Commons*
75 Bottom *Aylesham History*
Oakhill Brewery
79 Bottom *J A Peden*
81 Top *J A Peden*
Somerset & Dorset Joint Railway 84
Top *David Ingham – Wikipedia Commons*
84 Bottom *Andrew Fewster*
85 Top *David Ingham – Wikipedia Commons*
86 Top *John Collington – North Dorset Railway*
87 Bottom *John Collington – North Dorset Railway*
West Somerset Mineral Railway
91 Bottom *Unkown*
92 Top *Herbert Hole*
92 Bottom *Unknown*
93 Top *Unknown*
94 Bottom *Unknown*
West Somerset Railway
97 Top *Ben Brooksbank – Wikimedia Commons*
97 Bottom *A N M Gary – Creative Commons*
98 Top *A N M Gary – Creative Commons*
Yorkshire
110 Top *Andy Beecroft*
111 Top *Pocklington History Group*
111 Bottom *Pocklington History Group*
112 Top *East Riding Archives*
112 Bottom *Unknown*
113 Bottom *J D Stockwell*
114 Top *Glynnis Frith*
114 Bottom *Steven Large*
115 Top *Pablo York*
116 Top *Ken Nelson*
116 Bottom *David J Mitchell*
117 Top *David J Mitchell*
117 Bottom *J D Stockwell*
118 Bottom *Unknown*

119 Both *Unknown*
120 Top *Unknown*
120 Bottom *John Alsop*
127 Top *Unknown*
127 Bottom *Vic Nevell*
129 Bottom *Dr. W R Mitchell MBE*
130 Top *Historical Railway Society*
130 Bottom *Dr. W R Mitchell*
131 Top *Tarmac*
132 Top *Tarmac*
132 Bottom *Tarmac*
133 Top *Tarmac*
133 Bottom *Vic Nevell*
134 Top *Vic Nevell*
136 Bottom *Col. Stephens Railway Museum (CSRM)*
137 Both *(CSRM)*
138 Both *(CSRM)*
139 Both *(CSRM)*
143 Both *Swannington Heritage Trust*
146 Middle *Evan – Wikipedia Common*
146 Bottom *John Sloane*
148 Bottom *Chris Evans – Disused stations*
149 Top *Hampshire Airfields*
150 Top *Mike Morant Collection*
150 Bottom *Simplon Postcards*
152 Top *Alan Dingley*
154 Top *Secret Pilgrim*
154 Bottom *David Dixon*
156 Top *Maritime Transport – Craig Pusey*
156 Bottom *Maritime Transport – Craig Pusey*
157 Top *Network Rail*
160 Both *Halesworth to Southwold*
162 Both *Halesworth to Southwold*
163 Both *Halesworth to Southwold*
164 All *Halesworth to Southwold*
165 Top *Halesworth to Southwold*
167 Top *Glen Fairweather*
168 Both *Glen Fairweather*
169 Both *Eastleigh Lakeside Steam Railway*
175 Top *Hugh Llewelwyn – Wikipedia Commons*
176   Both *Peter Sedges*
178   Top *Lamberhurst – Wikipedia Commons*
178   Bottom *Phil Richards*
180   Both *Forth Ports*